It's not what you are

It's what you can be.....

...God is my dearest friend
and we look after each other

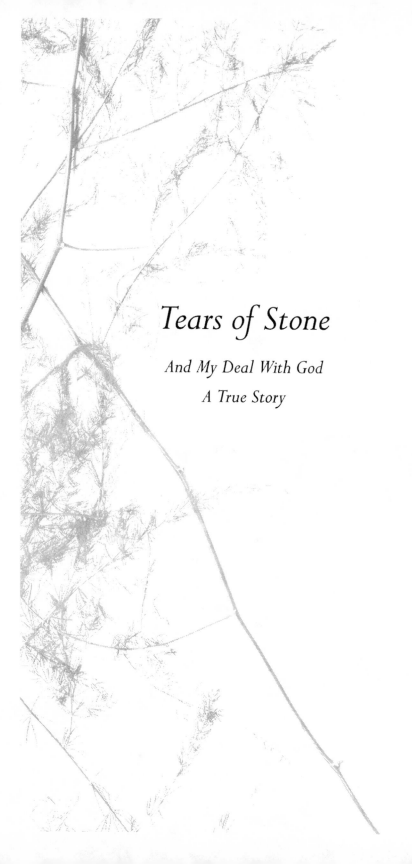

Tears of Stone

And My Deal With God

A True Story

First Edition

ISBN 0-615-28634-8

Published by Estherleon Schwartz

Contact: estherleon@estherleon.com
www.estherleon.com

Cover photograph by Ivor Pyres

Book design and typesetting by Michael Rosen

Printed in the United States of America

To Ivor

*In 1948, a little girl seven years old came to America with her mother
and father on the Queen Mary, with hundreds of other refugees.
Nearing the shores of New York, she saw a tiny statue in the water.
Everyone on the boat became very quiet and started softly singing
prayers of gratitude, kneeling down to kiss the ground.*

*The little girl couldn't stop looking at the beautiful statue in the ocean.
As they got closer and closer, it seemed as if this beautiful woman
with a wand, so tall and strong, was smiling at her and saying,*

"You are safe. You are in America."
*It reminded her of their escape, being chased by the Nazis in 1944,
and when her father threw her over the barbed-wire fence
at the Swiss border. Looking up to the heavens he said,
"Save my daughter and she will always serve you."*

*This little girl always knew in her heart,
her God-given destiny had been chosen....*

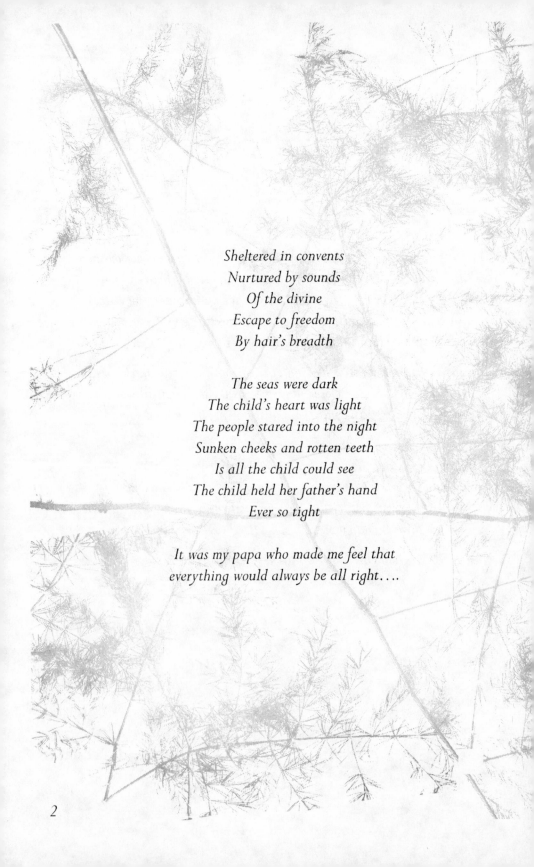

Sheltered in convents
Nurtured by sounds
Of the divine
Escape to freedom
By hair's breadth

The seas were dark
The child's heart was light
The people stared into the night
Sunken cheeks and rotten teeth
Is all the child could see
The child held her father's hand
Ever so tight

It was my papa who made me feel that
everything would always be all right....

The sky was blue
Almost too good to be true,
Could this be Papa's prayers
to heaven coming true?

The wand touches my lips
Sparkling sounds drip down my throat.
Papa squeezes my hand,
He looks at me
I look at him.
We knew everything was different
And what happened
So far away

7 years old

The Crown,
The Wand
The Red Dress
I always wanted to wear...
A tremor deep inside
Not like the other times on the run
Never seeing the sun
Where have I been....

Now, far away from the Swiss border, I still remember my father throwing me over the barbed-wire fence in 1944 into the hands of the Swiss soldiers. Even though I was only three years old and scared, I felt my father's words. These words would be imprinted in my heart forever.

The people knelt down
And kissed the ground
Whimpering sounds
Of prayerful music
That I always loved
Holding on to my papa
Was enough for me

Papa picked me up and held me tight. I felt the warm teardrops on my cheek.
They were not mine.

I always so loved to hear my father tell me the story of our escape when we were on the run and of my birth. It didn't matter to me if it was the millionth time or how old I was; to me, it was like the first time. The whole expression on his face and voice changed as if he was reliving and acting out each moment.

"Esty, your mother was so beautiful; she was Miss Vienna. We were separated by the SS on a train and put into different detention camps in the south of France under German occupation. We made a pact: If we escaped, we would wait for each other at a small post office on Fridays in a nearby village.... Your mother was about to be transported from Gurs detention camp to a concentration camp, when a young French captain pulled her out of the line and helped her to escape."

At that point, my father would sometimes pause and look deeply into my eyes in his quiet way, when he talked about her escape. I felt he was uncertain about carrying on the story, but I was so eager for him to continue that I would rush to him and say, "Don't stop, Papa, don't stop...."

He would pick me up and whisper into my ear, "You will always be my Esty." He would sit me down and continue the story, "Weeks and weeks went by, and then she saw me walk into the post office. Your mother did not recognize me, Esty. I was very thin and frail."

My Father, Leon Maurice Schwartz
Poland 1939

My Mother, Rose Schwartz
Vienna, Austria 1939

"You were born in Marseille, France, in 1941. It was night, there was nobody around. It was raining hard, loud planes in the sky.... Your mother couldn't make it anymore, Esty, she was about to have you.... She sat beside a garbage can in a dirty alley. I didn't know where to go, what to do, they wouldn't let us into the hospital——we were JEWS! I saw a church and banged on the door. AIDEZ MOI, AIDEZ MOI.

"A nun came out. 'Shh, Monsieur s'il vous plait, do not make noise.'

"I said to the nun, 'COME! MY WIFE IS HAVING BABY.' The nun came with me and we ran to your mother. She was lying on the ground, soaking wet. 'OH MY GOD MONSIEUR, bring her inside VITE!'

"I picked your mother up and walked quickly to the convent. I laid her down on the bed and she screamed. The nuns came over and surrounded your mother so I couldn't see her. I walked away to a corner and lit a cigarette. I was afraid for your mother, Esty, you were very premature...loud planes...the nuns blew out the candles. Everything went dark. Then I heard your beautiful voice crying.

"The nuns relit the candles, wrapped you up, and gave you to your mother, 'Here, Madame.' Your mother put her hand up and shouted, 'NEIN, NEIN—NON, NON.' They looked at me and walked over and put you in my arms. You were so small, so beautiful, my Esty."

Why would my mother not want to hold me first?

New York—1948

We were in America, big bold America as shiny as a dime and crisp as a new dollar bill waiting to hug us, but we were refugees with hand-me-downs and long boot laces, which we had to pull up to become who we wanted to be. Who we were made the difference and we kept on tripping and stumbling, but kept on pulling our laces up.

Tonight is Shabbas
I wake up early
Today is different
Can't explain why
Feels like magic in the air
Could it be the chicken soup I smell?

Walking up and down Brooklyn streets
People dressed up in their best clothes
Bow and say: "Good Shabbas."
Everyone seems happy

My uncle Moishe—my father's brother—his wife, Rebecca, and their
daughter, Sarah, were seated at the Shabbas table so beautifully
dressed. To me, everything and everybody sparkled.
Uncle Moishe, with a very gentle tone, spoke to me in French.
He asked me to sing the Shabbas prayer, as my aunt Rebecca lit the candles. I
sat next to my papa and was waiting for my mother to join us.
I stared into the lighting of the candles.

My mother was standing by the kitchen door looking at all of us.
Uncle Moishe began to pray, "Thank you, my loving, compassionate God."
My mother shouted, "YOUR COMPASSIONATE GOTT, WHO VATCHED
CHILDREN AND MOTHERS BEING GASSED? VHERE VAS YOUR GOTT
FOR ALL THE ONES WHO PUT ALL THEIR LOVE AND FAITH IN HIM?"
My father sadly looked at me. He could see the fear in my eyes and said,
"Rosal, it wasn't God's fault; it's the evil seed in some people."
My father and Uncle Moishe were getting upset.

I fearfully asked my mother, "Don't you believe in God?"

"Look at the candles, Esty. Vat you see?

Gott, or Hitler? Hitler or Gott? Huh, vat you see, vat you see, Esty?"

I looked at my papa and answered in confusion,
"I don't know! I love God, Mommy!"

My father pointed at my mother,
"ROSAL! Don't do that! You are scaring her."

It was the first time I heard my papa angrily saying something to her in this
shaky, loud voice. I blew out the candles, ran into the bathroom and threw up.

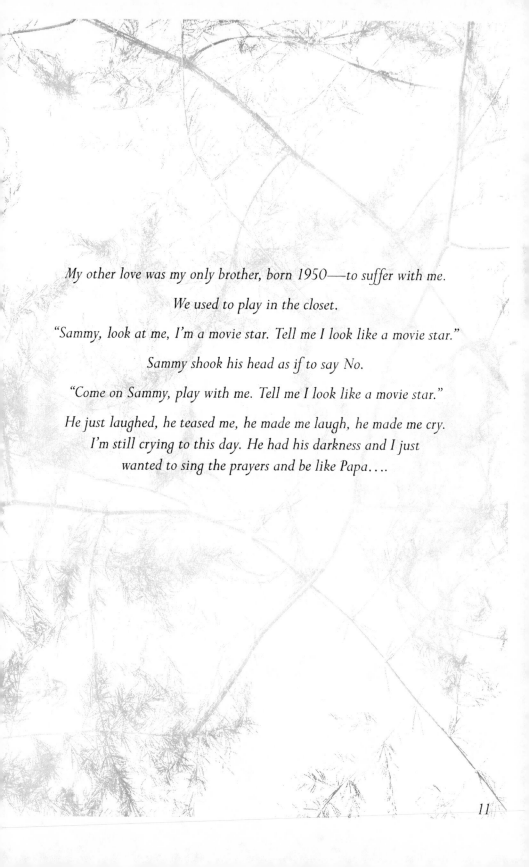

My other love was my only brother, born 1950—to suffer with me.

We used to play in the closet.

"Sammy, look at me, I'm a movie star. Tell me I look like a movie star."

Sammy shook his head as if to say No.

"Come on Sammy, play with me. Tell me I look like a movie star."

He just laughed, he teased me, he made me laugh, he made me cry.
I'm still crying to this day. He had his darkness and I just
wanted to sing the prayers and be like Papa....

11 years old

After school I couldn't play with my friends. I had to put snaps on baby clothing made by my mother in the garage on a sewing machine....
I started singing to myself, "Frère Jacques, frère Jacques, dormez vous?
"Vhy you sing?"
"Choir tryouts tomorrow, Mom."
"But you kan't sing."
"I love to sing. Remember, Daddy taught me the Sabbath prayer."
"DIS NOT SINGING."
"But, Mommy!"
"So, sing."
I began to sing but only a squeak came out.
"See, I told you. Just put snaps in. Don't vaste time."

In school, I wanted to belong and be part of everything. As a stranger, those years were very painful to me. Children didn't accept me, calling me a "green horn" (still don't know what it means, but it still hurts). I wanted so badly to get close to the music and sing in the school choir. I finally got a chance to try out, but when it was my turn, I started to shake. An ugly croaking sound was the only thing that came out and everyone laughed. I felt so ashamed, didn't sing again. (Except in my dreams and in the closet.)

Children don't understand

My mother doesn't understand

Ninth grade in high school, clothed in hand me downs from second-hand stores (not chic then). Rolling eyes from the cashmere queens and pinky rings, staring at me and whispering as I shyly walked the school grounds.

I always knew
One day things would be different,
I always had to remind myself
Who my real best friend was
But it was painful
Couldn't speak English well
Couldn't express myself
In any form
Felt like an outcast
Just didn't fit in
Except in my heart.
I kept reminding myself
Who is my real best friend
Who I could talk to day and night?
Don't need cashmere queens
And pinky rings,
I'd rather be with second-hand me

1961

*Can't imagine why my mother and orthodox father locked me up in my room,
when I told them on the night of my high school graduation that I was getting
married (first man I kissed). So I ran away from home and had two children,
ate peanut-butter-and-jelly sandwiches for dinner.*

*I always wanted children
I was as happy as a lark
Finally someone to hold,
Someone to pamper
Something to give me worth
Something to live for
Their names are:
Carrie (named after our favorite pizza place)
David (named after my father's brother
Who was gassed in Auschwitz)*

1966

Oh well, maybe my mother and father should have locked me up in my room, better yet in my closet and bolted it. I am left with two children, on welfare, in a cockroach-infested apartment on the south side of Beverly Hills (anything to ensure the kids would get a good education).

Roses are red
Violets are blue
Another disappointment in delirious love
That I thought had come true
Had to justify to my mother
Who warned me through and through
Don't want to face her,
Because I could become permanently blue

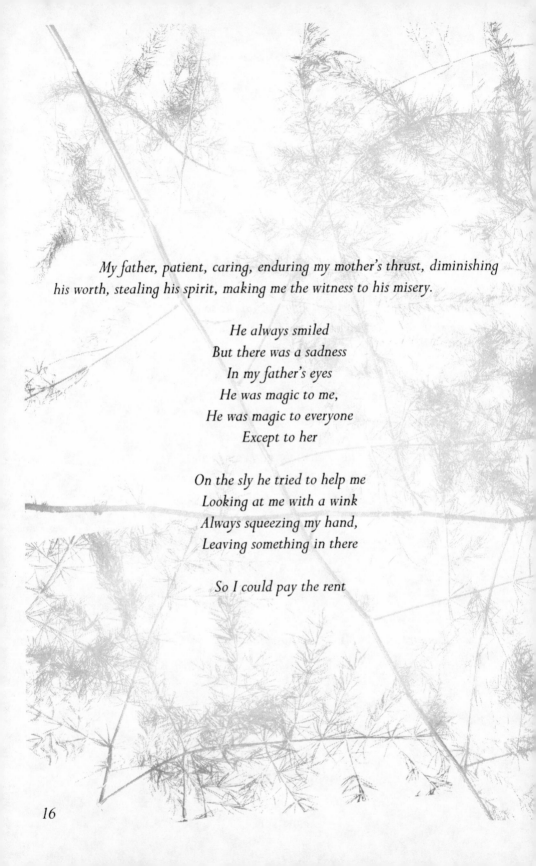

My father, patient, caring, enduring my mother's thrust, diminishing his worth, stealing his spirit, making me the witness to his misery.

He always smiled
But there was a sadness
In my father's eyes
He was magic to me,
He was magic to everyone
Except to her

On the sly he tried to help me
Looking at me with a wink
Always squeezing my hand,
Leaving something in there

So I could pay the rent

1973

*My dad was diagnosed with cancer. It didn't really register with me. When it
finally did, it was too late for me to have cared for him in that special way.
I remember he loved the brisket plate at the kosher restaurant on Fairfax.
I ran to bring two plates of brisket home for him. She (my mother) scolded me,
"You didn't ask me first."
He wasn't hungry anymore.
It makes me want to cry as I am writing this 35 years later—still hurts.*

*I am numb
I am a machine
I feel nothing
I died*

My everything is gone – the one who made me feel that everything
would always be all right

My everything is gone – the one who made me feel that everything would always be all right

My everything is gone – the one who made me feel that everything would always be all right

My everything is gone – the one who made me feel that everything would always be all right

My everything is gone – the one who made me feel that everything would always be all right

It was all my friends' goals, to have me married to a rich man by 30:
"You need to compromise, you still look hot, but soon you'll have to
cut off that long hair and look like the rest of us.
Your Delilah-and-Samson days will be over.
And how much longer with that Pinto that you park ten blocks
away from any party you go to, AND how about the blond wig
and dark shades that you pull out from under the back seat
of the car before walking into the grocery store.
"Oh, no, not again, Mom!"
Always hoping I would not be recognized, for Carrie and David's sake.
And the clincher—food stamps.

Dragged to parties
North side of Beverly Hills
Like a voyeur
Well-meaning friends
Delusions of grandeur,
Maybe it's me
Holding on to my ideals
Of romantic love
Sent from above

One year after my father's passing,
my mother was dragging me to Myron's Ballroom.

"Time for romance, Esty. Lets go dantzing.
I been goot for vone year.
"You too, Esty, can find new husband."

Even though I was sickened by her words, I now realize
that perhaps what she longed for was stolen from her
— the fulfillment of romance that nurtures the essence of a woman.

It was one-sided romantic love (for some that works).
It was the war. She was so beautiful, so she did what
she had to do. She knew my father since her teens;
he loved her at first sight and he was a good man.

As she danced with strange men, I could see them fall for her,
she was free. Could she have maybe...the captain, the escape....
Weeks and weeks went by (where was she?)...that look in my father's eyes
when he told me the story.... I looked at my mother on the dance floor;
she smiled at me. I was distracted from my thoughts. I held back tears
and felt sorry for her for the first time. I could never imagine
anybody but my father dancing with her or loving her more deeply.

So, in 1975, I did what I had to do; worked jobs that were not me.
My pre-teen kids were beating each other up,
and calling me every two minutes at work,
which ensured me losing every job (at least once a week).

Shall I compromise my ideals and surrender to temptation?
morals and values that people died for while standing tall?
being humiliated and made so small?
shall I compromise my Soul to the Devil and Angel?

questioning my reason and body parts to expose
a kept woman, in repose?
and what about Papa's soft eyes that kept me alive

What is my truth?
What is my purpose?
Only to survive?

demons, dark clouds that say:
new tennis shoes for David, braces for Carrie,
and a buck or two they'll have to carry
full of goodies you never bought

eviction notices and peanut butter
sandwiches for "din-din," will be of the past

come on, Esther, give yourself a rest
I'll choose your clientele; me Devil, me know best

In between the parties and the manhunts, I thought about my
father and what he would have thought. I had spared him the details.

I was invited to one of those fancy parties, tabloids and all,
by well-meaning friends. My best girlfriend, Trudy,
surprised me for my birthday with this most beautiful, vintage,
lavender shirt-maker dress and said, "Put on those sexy black strapless high
heels; that's all you need—something good is going to happen."
(She must know that lavender is a spiritual color; she picked it and is
the only one in the group who makes chicken soup.)

Walked into the room, shyly felt their stares
people coming over
going on and on with empty glares,
how long must I bear?
What's your name? What's your game?
is all they asked
Idle chatter on their sleeves
distant believers in reprieve
Polite me and
"No thank you's"
was my aim
to tainted hearts
that play those soulless games
Always remembering
one day things will be different
but when?
Still with illusions
To be with my soulmate

The husband of the host floated gracefully over to me and said
with a sheepish smile, "You've got to leave."
I asked, "Why?"

"You're upstaging my wife. Your dress, it's too beautiful."

"IT'S FOR SALE!" (I think I shouted.)

"What do you mean?" he asked.

"It's for sale!" I did my twirl. "It will look even more
beautiful on your wife and she's a blond."

"How much?" "$500" "You must be kidding."

I did my twirl again (girls, you should've seen this "cat" [meow] walk).
"Okay."
He thought he was paying for what was in the dress. (It pays to have a good
display when you're selling something, especially a one of a kind.)
(To ensure my kids had food, I would sell anything
— anything but you know what.
Trudy winked and squeezed my hand, I went for it, flew to the bathroom
and wore his monogrammed bathrobe home with five $100 bills in cash!
(In the '70s, that was a blessing.)
She told me later, with a big smile, my birthday present (the lavender shirt-
dress) had cost $45 In fact, it was a double blessing — the $500 too!
Anything means yer body, too.)
We looked at each other, she knew, and gave me the address.
And, of course, me, Goody Two Shoes, returned his
expensive bathrobe, leaving it on his doorstep.

I ran and changed those five, beautiful, gorgeous $100 bills into ones, they looked like a bouquet of green leaves, like manna from Heaven...to buy more of those lavender goodies. So the business side of me that I didn't know I had, said, "YES, YES, YES!" My living room in my cockroach-infested apartment became my boutique. Limos and Jags became my new clientele, instead.
I always held on to the words, "One day, things will be different."

Twists and turns
One never knows

How one's life
Could change
In an instant

It's hard to
Believe all these
Clichés
When you're desperate

I learned they
Help
If only for
An instant....

*I told my brother, Sam, about my new venture and he ran right over to check
me out! Compulsive, obsessive, in his elevator shoes, but brilliant and
entrepreneurial, always charming the world and women with his
Jack Nicholson shtick—that was my brother, Sam. He had a small
discount-clothing store (more like a swap meet) on Sunset Boulevard
in Hollywood, with his beautiful young Pakistani wife of a few years.
His two sons, dark skin, dark eyes, and dark hair were breathtaking.
Her father was like a father to Sam. The family adored him and
so looked up to him. When they divorced, I was heartbroken.*

*After a few years, out of nowhere, Sam introduces me to his next new wife,
with her young child and says, "Isn't she beautiful?" She was Chinese, yes,
lovely and very different from his ex-wife. Both women were very special in
their own ways. I ended up being in the middle, to keep peace,
as we all had a share in the Cashmere stores. Sam was now playing
a lot of Mahjong with her family, who looked to him
as the Golden Boy, and baby-sitting their newborn
baby boy. He was a beautiful mix and I, too, baby-sat him.*

*But Sam needed more; approval for his business empire from
our mother and the family of famed musicians, doctors,
lawyers; approval for his hilltop home, his car, his new slick
hairdo, sometimes straight, sometimes perm'd (we shared that
part, the hair). Yes, they Googled him alright, with their heathen
smiles, and a toast to the "SCHMATA MAN," (you know, the Rag Man).*

Words that sting
Words that burn
Words that destroy
The gentle Heart
Of a being
A kind-meaning word
Or none at all
Would be better
Than the words
That steal the breath
Of one
If not all

1979

So Sam said, "Sweet Sis, let's open a store and be partners."
I said, "Okay, Sweet Brother Sam, but only in Beverly Hills,
no swap meets for me."
Sure enough, hours later (for real), we opened the first silk-and-cashmere store
on Brighton Way in BH (Sam did his shtick with the landlord
and magic happened) with the "DISCOUNT" signs written
on toilet paper in the windows. Sam would grab anything handy
to put in the window with Scotch tape—
"Discounts! Going Out FOR Business"
Clever Sam invented those devious words.

Inspectors walking by—why should they care? Well,
they did and all the Rodeo Drive Gucci-ites came down
on us and said we were destroying their image.

And, sure enough the media came to our rescue and billed us as the
"CASHMERE BROTHER AND SISTER DUO—FROM RAGS TO RICHES"

For seven years, Sam and I were on top of the world, as the saying goes. The Pinto turned into a classic Mercedes Benz, the cockroach-infested apartment on the south side of Beverly Hills turned into a Malibu home on the beach. Carrie, David, and I all lived together in the world I had dreamed of. Sure, the first few months were exciting, waking up feeling you can touch the sky. But, after looking at the ocean for weeks and months and years, I got depressed, everything seemed so far away....

If those were my prayers
To heaven coming true

I must be delusional in my view
Sinking into the warm sand
Looking straight up Into the ice-blue sky

What's wrong with me?
I feel like I'm not alive
Perhaps, my deepest wishes never addressed
The inner holocaust with my mother
Never put to rest

The soulful prayers I knew that I haven't sung
To serve, to give is haunting me now all around

An empty feeling now exists
Flashing moments of my father's words
"Save my daughter and she will
Serve you forever"
Is all I heard.

December 5, 1985, on my birthday was the last time I spoke to my
brother, when he said, "Sis, we're going to celebrate your birthday later."
Later never came. With 11 House of Cashmere Stores on the rise,
my only brother, my best friend, was driven to take his own life.
—— I am alone. Now my two dearest loves, the ones I gauged all
my loves by were gone and no one could take their place.

If only I knew you were feeling so blue
I'd've been there in a heartbeat for you

If only I knew the pain you were in
I'd've been there in a whim

Put on my wings, soar thru the sky
Didn't know you wanted to die, you wanted to die

What does it take to feel that way
Disappointments that wouldn't go away

A love affair that didn't fare
A final decision that you didn't share

A tormented you that nobody knew
But I'm a big part of you

If only I knew that you're okay
Perhaps some of that pain would go away

It wasn't fair to leave that way
To leave me in pain each moment of the day

—— Lyrics from my album "Respectfully Different"—"If Only" (my song to Sam)

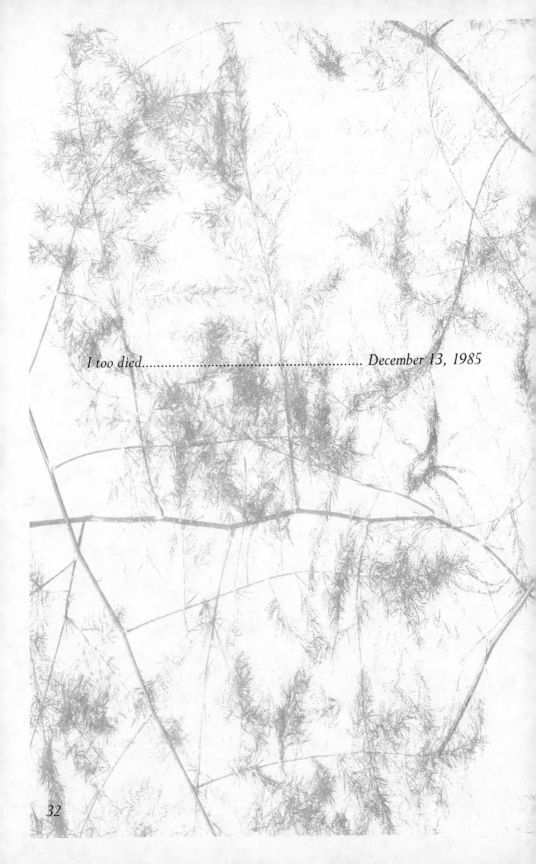

I too died.. December 13, 1985

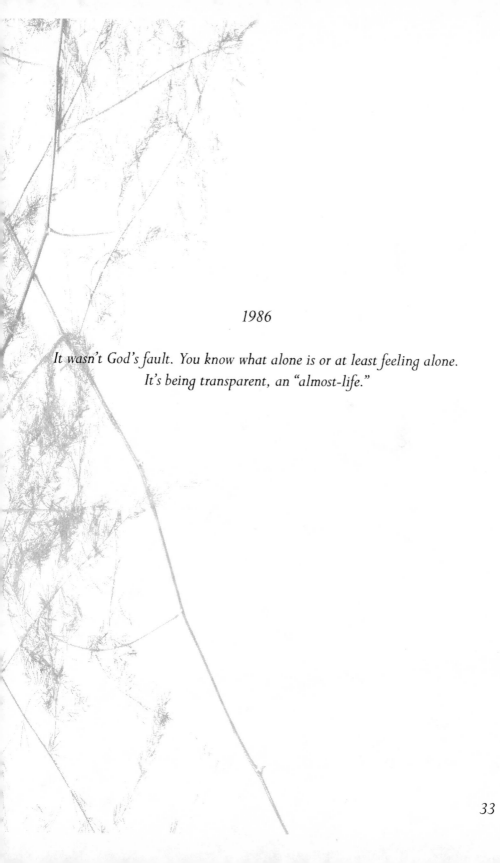

1986

It wasn't God's fault. You know what alone is or at least feeling alone.
It's being transparent, an "almost-life."

1987

The years pass by painfully, can't talk, can't write, can't anything....

Where's that mother of mine?

1988

"Now what, God?"

1989

Do something, Esther, pray, ask for a sign…Sam….

1990—Yom Kippur

I walked into our temple where my mother, father, Sam, and the
kids and I, used to sit in the seventh row, ever since we came to America.
The same Rabbi now seemed to be slumping over; I wondered if
he was ill. He always had something good to say, but it was hard
to understand him. His accent was really heavy, I mean
really heavy duty, but he was familiar, and it was like being
there again with everybody, just in a different way.
My heart seemed less heavy, even if just for
a little while.... I thought about Sam. If only I had
known how darkness had plagued him, cursed
with trying to prove himself, especially to our mother.

She said, "He had a sickness, Esty."
"Yes, YOU were his sickness," I yelled back.

I was almost tempted to tell her the truth,
(she thought it had been a car accident——I wanted to spare her).

I think she knew how he died. After all, a mother just knows
when her child is hurting...doesn't she?

*I was really missing Sam a lot. The only thing that gave me some solace
(believe it or not) was my long-time relationship with Sidney Sheldon's books
of Love, Power, and Sex. After an emotionally uninvolved day in my
cashmere store, I looked forward to coming home, chilling out with my
Oreo Cookies (you know, the dark-chocolate effect) and my mindless book.
One evening, as I was reading in bed, a brilliant-colored gold book
on my shelf caught my eye, as if saying; "I've been waiting for you."
It was a strange feeling, a feeling I was familiar with, like déjà vu.
It was haunting me.*

*Sorry,
Love, Power, and Sex
It's over
Nothing lasts forever*

*The Gold Book
Is my new romance
It has me hooked*

*Eating sleeping running
Dreaming walking talking
It's keeping me alive*

*The Holy Scriptures
Is now my life*

Now Barnes & Noble, The Bodhi Tree, and Borders bookstores became my
favorite refuge, where I spent hours of solitude for nourishment.
If I could have traded all my cashmere stores for one bookstore,
I think I would have healed sooner.
I filled my shelves with books I never had time to read—that didn't matter.
I knew that some day they would come into play. Just being surrounded
by authors of spiritual writings became the essence of my well being.
(I think it's called osmosis.)

A mission, a vision
Revealing my purpose to truth
The time has come

I read it in The Gold Book
Yes, in awe

Something I never really
Gave attention to

My awe
Your awe
World awe
One source

Soon my life will not live
In remorse —

Today is unraveling
God is good

These were the revelations I wanted to share with my mother, and did,
in spite of it all. She listened and stared at me blankly and said,
"You're a dreamer just like your father; get real or you vill
lose your cashmere stores—and don't come to me.
I varned you about your children's father.
And now I warn you again: SHUT UP vith your Gott."

Why did my mother behave like that? I was an enemy, a world
distant from my being. My mother's eyes were vacant. Who did
she see when she looked at me...? I was her child, wasn't I?

Poor woman of stolen soul
Poor woman, a heart that's mold

Poor woman of no hope
Dear God, bring her back

She's your lost child with a broken back
Give breath to her living death

She's still my mother; it's hard to rest
I cannot laugh, I cannot cry

Tears of stone
She's still my mother. . . .

Esther... (not again, that idle chatter)

take a breath

say some prayers

talk to God

and you will see

hold on to your faith,

Esther

unexplainable

magical moments

revealing

your calling

in this life

1991 – Friday – At temple, prophecy to transformation...

When I heard the Cantor davening (praying), my father's words and the sounds of the church music came back to me once again. My heart yearned to be up on the pulpit and be the female version of the Cantor, singing those haunting, soulful melodies. It drew me into a world of bliss and I wanted to stay there.

I didn't know Hebrew, the liturgy, or the melodies, but in my heart I knew them. So I made an appointment with a very famous Cantor at 9 a.m. the next morning. He asked me to sing The Star-Spangled Banner. By 9:05 I was standing outside his door holding back the tears...that croak in my throat had done me in again. Outside his corridor, I heard the beautiful voices as I had in the churches when I was on the run. Now I hear the choir in the chapel where I want to be. Fear (Satan) laughed in my throat, "Go back to your cashmere business." (Are Satan and my mother in cahoots?)

The secretary looked at me in sympathy, "Up the hill is a very well known Cantor, who might help you." So this Cantor #2 phoned Cantor #3, Cantor Mendelsohn, his mentor of 60 years, retired, living in the valley in Los Angeles (better known as Studio City). I prayed as I drove there in my new Maserati. I mean I really, really, really prayed, just like back in my Pinto days. His apartment was #11, a good sign...one of my lucky numbers. (My dad wore 4711 cologne.) I knocked on his door, held my breath, stood up straight, prayer in my mind, in my throat, on my lips. A little man in his 70s greeted me with a smile and those blue eyes, "So you vanta be a Cantor?"

He took me to the piano, played the scale, and said real loud, "SING TO ME!" (I think maybe he thought he was the main character of Phantom of the Opera.)

Sounds came out that I knew were always there. Before I stopped singing, seven other small-framed Cantors (all men) appeared and huddled around me as if I were an alien. "BRAVO!" they shouted, "at last, God has sent us a rare diamond." (With lots of baggage, I thought.) I asked him to call my mother. "You joke. My daughter vants to be a Cantor? You got to have beautiful voice."

"Your daughter is gifted; her voice brings people closer to God. Be happy."

She later shouted at me, "HE ONLY VANTED YOUR MONEY."

I said, "He never asked...."

Day in, day out, for months I learned the Hebrew language and Cantorial music. It was amazing the effect the Hebrew letters had on my soul. The letters were so beautiful that I knew I was talking to God. My Cantor would come to my Malibu home and climb thirty stairs to my door—panting!

"Oy Gevalt!" he smiled at me, "you worth it."

He said all the things I longed to hear from my mother. He also told me I had a form of ADD. (Oh, goody, now what?)

It worked to my advantage, as anything hard to learn was easy and anything easy to learn was hard for me. I didn't question his evaluation. All I cared about was that he saw the gift in me, even through my deficiencies. I always felt I was different and special in God's eyes.

Sam was the entrepreneurial genius behind the success of our stores.
The cashmere sweaters, made in our factories in China,
were distributed here in Los Angeles by Sam's U-Haul.

Oh well, I was fixated and obsessed with keeping the stores looking
"boutique-y" and inviting. One of my brother Sam's jobs was the banking.
When it came to finances and bookkeeping, my ADD and dyslexia
conveniently kicked in. Sam tried to explain simple concepts of finance
to me, and always had to repeat it three times and then I got it (sort of).
It became a joke between us. "Get it, Estycoo?" We laughed....

As my heart became a little lighter, thinking about it years later,
I looked up to the heavens and said, "Sammycoo, I need a SIGN
to know we are still connected—pretty please."

I was driving home from work in the rain and out of nowhere, a Sam's U-Haul
pulled in front of me. At first I thought it was just a coincidence; I shifted
lanes, it shifted lanes. My heart started to beat...okay, okay, okay! Give me
another two Sam's U-Hauls (you know, the "three thing") and sure enough,
one pulled up on each side of me. I was so taken and happy, because you
just know when there is divine intervention and I said, "Thank you, Sam."

Sam, still obsessed, was now sending me signs from everywhere.
His name popped up (in threes, of course). When I asked for a sign
or thought of him, that's when they appeared, and I knew this
was just for me, (even though everybody knows a Sam, I guess).
It reminded me of when we used to play hide-and-seek, when
we were kids—really poor—but happy to have each other.

I ran the hills early each day
In my hands, on my lips
The secret language of God
Now imprinted in my heart.
Eager to learn
Lucky me
It came so easy —
Was meant to be
Each word became my way
Made some of my pain go away
The words were magic
As if all is connected
A hope, a feeling
In the deepest part of me
Something magical
One can only feel, not see
Something unexplainable is happening to me

While dragging Carrie and David on Friday nights to Temple, I was saddened by the empty seats. I had to do something. After all, I felt I got "the blessing" I had to figure something out!

So I told my Cantor, "On Friday night, lets do a service in my home in Malibu on the deck, with lots of music and poetry under the heavens."

I invited 30 people, more than 150 showed up (word of mouth works the best). When everyone left, I stood on the deck over the ocean and called out,

"Thank you, God. NOW WHAT?!"

My conversations with God became more demanding; I wanted to know the next step. I actually had the gall to ask God to give me a sign, like, to reveal Himself. (I think I was still under the influence of that magical evening).

One must truly be careful what one asks for. Out of nowhere came a beaming light, like an arrow from the sky into the ocean and straight onto my deck. I was so startled, I ran into my house. It followed me straight into the kitchen through glass windows. I started to sweat, felt heart palpitations
—it went away, for a few minutes anyway.
I called my daughter, Carrie.
She worked in a restaurant by the ocean;
"Did you see the white beam in the sky?" I asked her.
"No, Mom."
I called my friend who lived by the ocean.
He said, "No. No light here."

Then the beam came back. I promised myself I would never ask God
again, as I knew I couldn't share this experience with anyone
(except you, now), because "they" would have put me
in a straitjacket and locked me up
(this was in the early '90s, before The X-Files).

So I asked,
So I received,
Perhaps not ready
To fully believe

A beaming white light
Staring me down,
Saying: I am here;
Don't be afraid

I'm always around,
So, ask for you,
Ask for all

Now and forever
Waiting for your call

Don't be afraid
You are the one,
One of the chosen....
(A done deal)

So…I started doing services in different venues for single people. It was always my wish to bring together all cultures and religions for a better understanding of one another; we have more in common than not…. Music is God's language, and singing the prayers became my way to communicate.

And there was standing room only!

In the receiving line after one service on Yom Kippur, people kissed my hands and gave me words of praise. My mother stood next to me with her sisters, and when someone complimented her on my behalf, she replied, "It's nice vat you say to my daughter; she tries so hard! But you know, she really has a successful cashmere business. Maybe she should stick to that." And her sisters smiled. (I knew that patronizing smile.)

I always prayed and hoped I could do my thingthat I felt was my calling of the heart, in spite of the dark forces sitting in the first row, staring me down. (Maybe it's my own insecurity.)

One day, I began my daily run up the hill around my home in Malibu.
Yes, still with the short shorts, T-shirt and all. This most
deer-like dog, better known as a German shepherd, appeared
out of nowhere and stared at me with his brownish, amber-colored,
soulful eyes. I never saw this dog before, yet it felt like he was part of me.
He kept looking at me as if he were trying to say something.

During the next two days, each time he appeared,
the same feeling came over me.
Then on the third day, a man came over and said, "When you do your run,
our dog jumps over this high fence. We cannot understand how he makes it
over! You can see how high it is." As he left, the dog would not budge.
When the man finally took him away, the dog's eyes never left mine.

The next day, the dog was on my doorstep. The owner came looking
for him and just said, "I don't know what's going on. Since he's seen
you, he is not the same dog and it's getting a bit strange."
"Yes, I know what you mean," I said. "What's your dog's name?"
"His name is Sam."

P.S. I renamed Sam, the dog, Samantha, as I didn't
know if my brother wanted to come back as a dog.

The signs were coming left and right
always in threes so clear and bright
feeling better, now that I know we're connected
it's you, me, Daddy, and Samantha
God has connected. . . .

Ruda, my long-time, devoted Russian employee, manager of my two stores in Beverly Hills, calls me: "Esther, darling, you must come in; we are low in merchandise. The rent is due and you are behind on payroll. And most of all, the store needs you! And your mother calls every hour to see if you came to work."

"Okay, okay, I'll call." I held my breath, said a prayer, and called my mother. This time she really, really, I mean really ragged and ragged on me and, in between, told me about her new up-do, her new Bulgarian boyfriend, an engineer with little money, but very romantic.

She forgot to ask about the kids and me—she can't help herself.

"My dear ones, my time has come, your time has come...." During the sermon for one of my services, I was so pleased to see the seats filled with people from all walks of life. I could sense their need, and I prayed that nothing would get in the way of my doing God's work. A part of me was totally in awe, and as I spoke I felt it wasn't me. It was and is the most out-of-body experience, sharing thoughts and beliefs so strongly, so passionately. People were actually listening and so quiet, a silence I had not experienced before.

In between the stillness, the words on my lips became sounds flowing out like water down a gentle stream. The Voice in my head kept saying, "Thank you, thank you, thank you." This moment of bliss made up for so many hours of pain.... As I was about to sing the Sabbath prayer, they walked in. Fear, my enemy, my mother and her entourage sat down in the front row, smack in front of me and just stared at me (that's what it felt like, anyway). My heart and stomach came up in my throat, "Oh no, please, please, keep the blessing going."

I tried so hard with all might to shake off the fear, the dark memories. Flashing colors were all I saw and I started to sweat

My Cantor, who trained me, was a witness to this pathetic moment that felt like eternity. He went down and told them to sit in the back, as those seats were reserved for the "press" (right!). He loved me; I was his singing angel, and he protected me like my brother and father would have.

"Sing my angel, the heavens are waiting to start the Sabbath."

I shook, I closed my eyes and saw God, and sang (not so great, I mean my singing).

It haunted me for days and days when I didn't make those divine sounds that I knew I could, and people thought, "That's it?" Once, I even overhead a conversation between some people arguing, saying, "She's wonderful and so inspirational." And their friend would argue, "You all need HEARING AIDS." I was so unpredictable. I had to do something to distract me from me....

So! I told my congregation, I had an idea that could serve us all well ("Not again!" I felt they were thinking). Yes, I had tons of ideas. Incorporating poetry into a service on the Sabbath seemed foreign to others. Me, I thought that was a no-brainer—a singles' service for them to meet their next new husbands (better known as doctors, lawyers, accountants, etc.) to introduce to their mothers under the auspices of holiness. Singles, who pray before they play....

Having had my cashmere stores in high-profile areas, it came to me, "Yes! Yes! Yes! a storefront spiritual kind of reading room/meeting place, books, art, music, people of all walks and colors of life to come in and, even if just for a minute, breathe in some divine-ness. I wanted to create a non-threatening, universal space of holiness, where all could come together to rejoice in the wonderment of life!

I continued, "READ MY LIPS," I said to my congregation,
("Gentler tone, Esther.") "I'm a dreamer; I'm a believer,
now and forever. Who is with me on this one?"

There were buts, 'what-ifs, how's, where's, and BUTS again....
Finally I stated my case, "Of course I understand that this idea
of a storefront spiritual reading room seems, oh well,
impossible perhaps to visualize or attain.

After all, no one else in the community who I know of has done this before
except Christian Scientists, with their storefront reading rooms, and they
are quite successful in keeping their message out there with easy access.

It seems to me—and just think about it?—why are there so many
empty seats in temple and why are people turning to others' spiritual
disciplines? "Where did that come from?" I thought to myself (not bad
for a Jewish girl just trying to do her thing). Still, the singing saga
haunted me. One day, things will be different.

Because I'm a believer...most of the time.

Twists and turns
One never knows
How life could change
With an instant thought
Followed by miracles

...And now, with all that said, NEXT!

*I drove around on Olympic Blvd. with "Sam-chatter" in my head.
When I saw this empty storefront in an atypical mall, it looked like
a temple with that Far East influence, it spoke to me. It had pillars,
trees, and a beautiful staircase. The actual storefront, empty, faced
the boulevard with heavy traffic and people walking by.*

*Sure enough, I guess when you're a dreamer, a believer,
unexplainable things happen. I think it's called '"faith in your fate"
or something like that. All I know is, it works, and not just for me....
I met the landlord and did the Sam-number on him. He didn't know
what he was in for. I pleaded poverty for our people of the world
and said, "Mr. Landlord, are we not all connected? You are the chosen
one to help humanity. Rent the place to me and you will be
very proud of your new tenants—MY CONGREGATION."*

*They were not just empty words. I think he understood after a while —
actually a long while, like a couple of minutes, which felt like forever.*

*Everything in its right time. "Just do the footwork, Esther."
That always made me feel better (talking to myself).*

*Yes, just say yes
I'm a dreamer
I'm a believer
stay in action
and you will see
unexplainable revelations
In the time it is meant to be.*

*This scenario and declaration from Up Above was now imprinted in my heart
and sealed with a lease for one year...in November, 1994.*

*December 5th, 1994, my birthday, I opened my first storefront spiritual center
for all peoples called "THE SHUL." And once again they came in droves,
and once again I had a chance to do something that could bring
people together for good reasons, more yet to be revealed.*

*A month of miracles
Chanukah and Christmas*

We were all still living in Malibu—my Carrie, David, and Samantha
(the dog). Carrie was working and going to school for nursing,
which I talked her into because of my flashbacks from
when she was nine years old. I watched her bring in stray birds and use
Popsicle sticks to mend their wings. I saw her feeding stray dogs, cats, and
hamsters with an eyedropper. She even used my personal hairbrush to
pretty up some poor, sweet, hairless dog she rescued and named Blackie—she
nurtured them all back to health. She even cleaned their cages herself. If
Carrie could've caught a fly and healed it, she would have; she had that
healing touch, and still does. I could see her destiny as a humanitarian. I,
too, once wanted to be a doctor, nurse, policeman, fireman to save people.

My David, I think, was still mad at me for being late for a casting call
for the Bad News Bears movie when he was 13 years old. He felt he had
missed his big chance in life, since he had been in the same class as Nicolas
Cage. I couldn't be in three places at the same time. So I was five minutes late,
work, welfare, timing. How could I know those five minutes would
change his life forever and the regrets all pointed at me?

David would wait by the window when he was three years old for
his father, my ex. He is still waiting, I think, and I'm still
doing the mother thing, especially when he calls and leans on me.

I never questioned my children's love, even when we only had peanut-butter
sandwiches for dinner in our cockroach-infested apartment. But on the south
side of Beverly Hills, trying to give them a better education, I tried....

Their friends and mine all lived on the north side, had ice- cream for dessert,
like at Baskin Robbins with toppings, instead of the 49¢ scoop at Thrifty's.

I was very happy to have my new storefront, a place that I could wake up in the morning excited to go to, that gave so much meaning to my life—this was my life. I ended up renting a room out in the Malibu house so that I could pay the mortgage and the rent (barely) and slept on a futon under the ark with the holy scriptures, the Torah looking at me, surrounded by the books I loved.

The walls were lined with contemporary spiritual art, the music was always on and, of course, fresh flowers. I took some of my clothes and belongings and hid them behind a screen; actually it was a beautiful, free-standing screen, like a movie prop, something like Queen Esther's hangout. No one knew, except you now reading this, that I slept there.

For some reason, there were more men than women attending. Usually the reverse; had to think quickly, as I was not available for what they were fantasizing. After a while, I guess they realized they were not going to be my sole soulmates, so they all disappeared and now I was left with mostly women, who hoped they would meet a good man to bring home to their mothers.

In the steam room at the gym, I overheard a beautiful blond with this gorgeous body, saying to another girl that she was going to a Shabbat service where there was a female Cantor who sang like a bird, with dark, long hair, sad eyes, and helped girls get off the beat. (I later figured it out.)

"Hey, that's me," I thought to myself. Now what? I had to think fast on my feet. "Sam, what would you do?"
Signs, yes, that's it, put up a sign in the window that says:

"MEET THE SPIRITUAL PLAYMATE OF YOUR DREAMS,
AND BRING HER HOME TO MAMA"
I asked the girls to "give up" with the bunny uniforms, and they now appeared with their new look—buttoned-up blouses and tennis shoes.
The police had to direct traffic as the limos and press pulled up.
It felt like the old days with Sam....

My mother's boyfriend, Yanesh, from Bulgaria, the engineer, now became her new husband. His eyes never left my mother's flirtatious, coy look and provocative gestures through her thick eye glasses. She never took her shaded glasses off. Glasses or not, it did not matter to him; she was his Rosie with the features of a deer, red lipstick, and bleached-blond hair. He sniffed her female essence and adored her like my father did.

With his Bulgarian accent and her Viennese accent, they chattered away and kept dancing to their own beat. That look of love, or maybe lust (good for them!) filled the room with bliss and a kind of hope.

I did like Yanesh; he was very sensitive, caring, and spiritual, the opposite of her. He loved my singing, the prayers, my poetry, and my words of the day. It was good for me to see her happy and smiling, with a red rose in her hair and red lipstick that gave her beautiful skin that lily-white look....

Just as I was settling into my spiritual storefront, which took about a year, the lease was up and my landlord wanted the place back. So here comes Sam's U-Haul again, until Steven Spielberg's Righteous Persons Foundation, and some of his friends, who also had foundations, came along and gave me some grants to save the day once again. Now I was on the Third Street Promenade, Santa Monica, California.

I was ahead of my time, as usual, serving people of all religions and walks of life. Once again, they came in droves, lit candles, and I said, "May God bless you and good-bye," knowing I might never see them again, not in this location anyway.

My heart was heavy and the media wrote stories, asking people to pray and save THE SHUL. It wasn't meant to be, and I wanted just to once again believe....

I was always ahead of my time in other ways as well. When everybody's hair was long, mine was short—the androgynous look; when the fashion was short, mine was long. They wore jeans; I wore silk dresses and spiked high heels. It was never intentional; it was just my expression at that time of life, or moment. I shopped in secondhand stores before it was chic and the in thing, first out of necessity, then by choice.

One of my special, mindless things to do is to get into bed, channel surf, open pistachios, and sometimes even make hot chocolate with, yes, half-and-half cream, against all prescribed rules (you know, cholesterol). Now my lavender-streaked hair is almost to my waist and my nails are longer than ever. And at my age—67—against all the odds!

My favorite programs were the preachers. Whenever I would hear them shout or sing praises to God, it was a quick fix for my soul. I mean sometimes this was like three o'clock in the morning and they put me back to sleep peaceful....

The uncertainty of not knowing where and how challenged my faith in a big way. Again, I started to spend most of my days at the usual bookstores, with my 3 zips of Starbucks, searching for inspirational titles to pick me up.

I thought of my precious things in a cold storage, after all, everything has a soul. Even inanimate objects (like toothpaste that reminds you to brush your teeth), has an energy and purpose. What's mine? What's yours?

I was becoming a philosophical warrior that made me search with passionate determination to find answers to my past, and to turn thoughts and my point of view into words that make sense for my existence.

P.S. I became my own think tank, like Sam.

P.P.S. If only Sam could have had enough time to explore the same blessings.

Esther's Revelations

You are the warrior

    of forgotten dreams

        who gives hope

            and restores faith...

                It is your word

                    your deeds

                        carry many afar

Carrie married a wonderful, Argentine man. She finally had the model husband, handsome, supportive, kind, and the best father of fathers to his children, including a model family of sisters, brothers, cousins, dogs, and one cat (I think) and of course, the model grandparents, always there for their children and grandchildren with candy and presents, and mucho love....

I was very happy for her and for me, knowing my princess was safe and in good hands. The only hurt for me was when Max, my first grandson was born, they moved to Florida. Then came Jordan, and my granddaughter, Danielle, who likes to be called Dani. Sure, I visited them, always gauging my trips around the other grandparents, not to intrude on them. I did feel like that at times.

I swallowed it and tried not to show my feelings. Poor Carrie, she was in the middle of this and said, "It's your own insecurities, Mom."

"Thanks," I thought.

"I mean how would you feel if every time your kid and grandkids came to visit from out of town and the whole gang is there and it's just me and I wait for my turn for a one-minute kiss 'n' hug and the kids are whisked off in an SUV to the valley, to a home where everyone has a bedroom, big fridge, and space to breathe? I watched as they waved bye-bye, threw kisses, especially Dani.

(Esther chatter, "You could've kept your SUV, you chose to trade it for a sports car that seats 1.5. You could've stayed in your Malibu three-story, beach-front pad, but you chose to parlay that into a four-plex, living in one of the three-bedroom units with the sacred room where the kids loved to hang out. Soon after, you chose once again to downsize yourself, from there to the *converted garage. All this to accommodate your mission in life.") In retrospect, these choices had repercussions——like longing to be closer to my family.)*

When it gets really bad and I miss them too much, I buy Skittles, their favorite candy, and B-B-Q potato chips, go to The Grove, sit by myself in a movie theater, and pretend I'm with them.

~

What I didn't know was that the kids argued with Carrie on the plane, because they wanted to come to my "hideout" in the back of my building that the kids thought was cool. The income from my apartment building would pay the mortgage. At least I could continue my outreach work and pay the costs of venues to do services in, the printing of flyers, yadda, yadda, yadda.

I think what the kids really loved were my God stories (that I made up) and that I had told them ever since they were born, when we all got into bed together and watched The Spy Who Shagged Me for the hundredth time, and oh, yes "Mini Me" and candy and buttered popcorn and soda, all that in my tiny bedroom, with one small bathroom. What a great movie!

By 2004, I had lots of bits and pieces of video footage of my life,
and wanted to edit it into a nice little story for my grandchildren to have
when I will be with my father and Sam in Heaven. So I called
the American Film Institute and asked if they could help me.
Someone replied very politely, but shortly and said,
"Lady, this is a film school. Check the Yellow Pages for editing."

I got off the phone and was frustrated. That afternoon, I got
a phone call from a man with an English accent: "This is Ivor Pyres
from the American Film Institute. I understand you need some help."

I was so surprised, like, almost in shock, as I never left my number.

Twist and Turns
One never knows
If only I could remember
This poetic thought
I would be less distraught
If only I could remember

I gave him ten days to make up his mind to bend the rules, and just
to see me, to guide me. I said, "Mr. Pyres, I'm a grandmother, have a heart,
and besides, God's listening to this conversation." He chuckled. You know,
the polite English manner, yet there was a gentleness in his voice.
It just had that poetic tone. I shared my giggle book with him that
went something like this: "Friends who giggle together, stay together.
Make a date and ask a friend to go giggling."

(It gets better....) He laughed, I mean we broke out into
that hysterical laughter, where you can't even say anything
because you can't stop laughing.
(Feels so good after a good laugh, doesn't it?) He thinks I'm funny, honey.

When I got off the phone, I started writing poetry.
I felt an excitement from long, long ago that I had forgotten.

~

Yanesh and my mother lived in Laguna Hills in a retirement community—resort-style living—tennis courts, swimming pools, saunas, dining and dancing. This had to be heaven for them and it was. My mother primped in her bathing suit, with her high heels, earrings, totally gussied up, strutting down the runway of the pool. Yanesh wore his chic tennis gear, strutting after her.

She always told me, with a big smile, how all the men came over to her, how they stared at her, and that Yanesh was very jealous, which made me uncomfortable for poor Yanesh and me.

This was only the beginning.... Yanesh had two beautiful daughters who he raised, and who now lived far away. They loved their papa so much, as I loved my papa. I loved when they came over and I saw how he loved them. I felt a lump in my throat and wanted to reminisce with my mother about my dad and Sam. I just wanted to crawl into bed with her and talk.

"Later," she said,

Later never came.

"Is God doing His thing'"

I walked up the circular staircase and was directed to Mr. Pyres' office.
I sat on a bench in the long corridor, looking at the posters of famous
movies and got just a little queasy. A man with beautiful dark skin, full
head of black hair, and cocker-spaniel eyes (you know, those soulful puppy eyes
that I like), came out and introduced himself...a smile to die for and the same
body type as Sam and my dad. He was very polite, said he would be
right back and then disappeared just as fast as he had appeared.
I waited for a few minutes and went to the bathroom to check out
my hair (it was a bad-hair day, girls), felt a bit insecure.

He came out and led me to a screening room. I gave him the video, he turned
the lights off, started the video, and sat next to me. I felt a little strange
(nervous is more honest), as I had not been in such close proximity to a man
in a long time. I had to get over this feeling fast, like in 20 seconds!

I remembered what my father said at the Swiss border: "Save my
daughter and she will always serve you." I made a deal with God
a long time ago, that if I had a choice to fall in love again
or do my work, I chose to do my work. (I'm already getting distracted.)
Be faithful to your work, Esther, I thought.

As I sat next to him, my feelings overcame me. The seats were so close
that if I turned to talk to him, his face was almost in my face!
It was so awkward, I think I wished I had never come here.
Maybe I should have listened and looked in the Yellow Pages
and how did he get my number? I never left it....

"Is God doing His thing?'
Sign time, Sam?"

My favorite day of the week has always been Friday. On Mondays, I look forward to Fridays, to light 13 candles for all my family and friends who are in Heaven. (The tradition is two candles; God understands my ways.)

As I light each candle, I talk to them—the candles and each member of family I miss so much through the candles. I feel, for real, everyone is present in an unexplainable way. One time, I asked the flames to wiggle and held my breath and they did; I'm sorry, there was not an adult witness. My granddaughter Dani, all of seven years old, my best witness for life and more, saw this. I always chose a special person in my life to pray for, who needed extra prayers. This time and most times it was my son, David.

It's hard for me to really, fully indulge in the joy of life, when my child is still hurting. Yes he is 39+, for me he is my David, who burned his tushie on the heater when he was three years old and when he hit that home run at seven years old and everybody cheered him except his father, who never knew.

Revelation

you are the loyal heart of adoration, who brings beauty of

pure spirit, showing true compassion and inspiration

who gives the world the best of you...

The beautiful brown-skinned man, Ivor, called me and asked me to meet him
at the airport. He had a surprise for me. He said he was leaving for
England for a couple of weeks to visit with his brothers (lucky him).

He was born in Bombay, India, Catholic, raised in England from
the age of ten. As I saw him at a distance, he kind of reminded me
of the late Pope John Paul, II, who I and everyone adored. His slow,
methodical walk, with his tweed overcoat just like my father wore,
this man named Ivor out of nowhere just reminded me of
my everything, my papa...there goes that lump in my throat.

And the worn, soulful eyes (it must be the India-persona thing)
the look of a wise man, only thing missing was a full head
of gray hair and a beard. Actually, I think he colored his hair;
in the sunlight it had that funny hue of red, you know
what I mean, especially when you use cheap dye (yes, it's the hair
thing again...one day when I'm over it, I will know I've arrived).

He surprised me with the video and said, "I hope you will be happy."
It was cold and windy. Between the tweed overcoat and the gray
hat out of the '40s, you know, the Humphrey Bogart look; all he needed
was a cigarette and feather in his hat. He looked the part; he was the part.

We politely hugged one another good-bye, felt awkward again, my hair blew
in my face and he gently pulled it aside. His hand touched my face.
My heart skipped a beat and I felt an excitement that I had buried.

Remember, I was God's bride....

By 1999, I had lost my House of Cashmere stores, one by one.
When people would ask me where's your partner,
your brother Sam, I said he moved to China. "If you go there,
tell him his sis says, 'I miss you.' He'll understand."

I left it alone. Felt alone. And more. Once again, my only refuge
was, you know, the bookstores, with 3 zips of coffee, searching...
searching for titles that would grab me enough to skim that book.

My eyes spoke to me from Kahlil Gibran, Wayne Dyer, Louise Hay,
on and on and, of course from the great, inspirational, theological
and biblical writings. All these hundreds of books now
on my shelves for me to inhale their wisdom,
the history of all nations, and stories of hope.
I felt I was part of all this (still do).

It soothed me as long as I kept myself isolated from
certain people from the past who I thought held me back
from a destiny, my destiny that I knew I had and wanted
to fulfill. It was a process: I had to learn that I am who I am.
Who I am would reveal itself, and it did, and it still does.

The kids were always in my heart and I missed them so much. David, my son and Mikey, his son, my grandson, both totally charismatic in their black garb, tall and gorgeous with their dark Armani shades, walking into my High Holy Days services and my other grandson, Jordan's bar mitzvah, heads turning, like something out of The Sopranos——I loved it! My Mikey, a young Desi Arnaz look-alike, a babe-magnet and a sushi lover, can charm you into anything, and is very protective of his Nana (his other grandmother), his mother, and me. "I love you's" were always on his lips. Mikey was now 17 years old. I remember when I first saw him, he took my breath away and still does.

David never married Mikey's mother. Mikey adored his mother to the point of tattooing her name across his arm, I suppose to always have her close by, in spite of everything. Her own mother more than helped raise Mikey. He was street wise, unlike cousins Max and Jordan, but they all have the same good hearts.

And even if I didn't see Mikey very often, I understood, but it did kind of hurt; he only lived 20 minutes away over the hill in the valley. There was always an excuse why our plans were broken——sometimes life got in the way. David and Mikey were going through tough times and I just wanted to be David's mother and Mikey's grandmother.

I'd say more I love you's
less I'm sorry's
and more I need you's
to really feel you
I'd say more thanks
and give more smiles
for all the beauty
that surrounds me
when I live
my life over again
with an understanding
there's something
greater that surrounds me
if I had another chance
I'd have more faith, take the risk
to play and dance to this life
when I live my life over again
searchin' hard to find the pieces
to fulfill my destiny
and if just for one more breath
I'd smell the roses
feel the raindrops
fall on my face
knowing
I had another chance

More "I love you's" from our album, Respectfully Different.

*Every time I saw their little faces, Max, Jordan, and Dani, when arriving
at the gate at the airport in Florida, I felt a sense of real, hard-core,
unconditional love. My grandchildren greeted me like your
dog greets you as if he hasn't seen you in a hundred years.*

*My Max, 18 years old, had that George Clooney look. Ever since he could talk,
if anyone looked at me in a "funny" way or said something that might have
hurt me, he would lash out without fear, even at his own parents. It was him
for me, me for him. He was my karate, black-belt security guard. The first
thing we always did when I visited them in Florida, is go straight to
to Coral Springs mall, just to walk around. It was and is our tradition.*

*My Jordan, creative, inquisitive, sensitive, looks like something
out of GQ with his cool dark shades. Every time I call and hear
his gentle voice, I melt and realize how much I miss him and everybody.
Recently, I told him about finishing my book and from this gentle voice
roared, "YAY!" He said he'd be the first to buy it. I shared with him my
longing for everyone and he came back with, "I understand your pain."
He's just a kid, 13 years old, but an old soul....*

*My daughter, Carrie's hug was sometimes mechanical. Yes, there are
times when she is really there; you just know when it means something.
Words only get in the way. Someday, things will be different.
She will understand and allow herself to feel my overwhelming
love for he; she is my princess, she is my Carrie.*

Maybe in time...(hopefully)

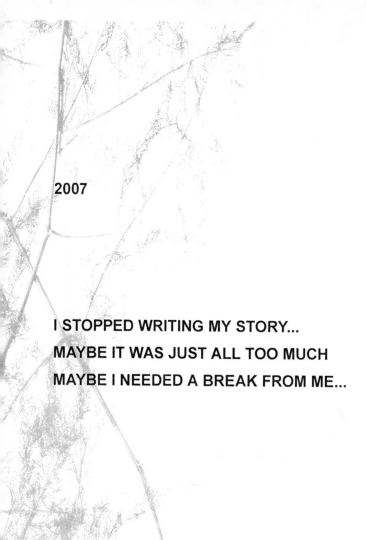

2007

I STOPPED WRITING MY STORY...
MAYBE IT WAS JUST ALL TOO MUCH
MAYBE I NEEDED A BREAK FROM ME...

Esther's Prayer

Should I go astray
bring me back
with kind words
to guide my way

Should I go astray
bring me back
to take in
another
God-given day

If I really go astray
remind me of me,
my family
my friends
there for me each day

And if I really, really
I mean really go astray
remind me

This too shall pass
and it does...

2008

As much as I thought about my life,nothing made me want to put pen to paper.

2009, JANUARY 20TH, TUESDAY, INAUGURATION DAY

OBAMA SWORN IN—THAT DID IT!

I thought back to when I came to America in 1948, a child Holocaust survivor and saw the Statue of Liberty.... That same feeling overcame me once again, the feeling of being safe and proud.... Yes, I'm back! Sharing my saga with you again.

Ivor, after doing my e-mails for four years, brought a stranger into my life—a one-eyed, fluorescent-blue IMac, better known as a computer. It sat in his office for eight months before I let go of my ADD and succumbed to learning how to use it. The blinking light on it drew me into what I considered The Twilight Zone, at this time of my life. When anything goes wrong, I still scream to him for help on the phone

What do I know? Seeing a blank Word document was my substitute for a psychiatrist, so once again, I started to write my story. On top of that, when I got up each morning, I felt my beloved, empty Word document was saying, "Hi, talk to me, talk to me." Is this too crazy, that I looked forward to seeing that empty page that somehow got filled up? It had to be the guided hand.

I am grateful for our newly restored pride, inspired by the shift in our country and the world. As I always said and truly felt, "Everything in its right time."

Tell me not that our new president was not Divine Intervention.

To my Linda, Ivor and Lisa-Catherine:

One simple opinion
From a caring friend
One simple opinion
From a gifted friend
One simple opinion
From that kind of friend
Can make the difference
At the end....
Choose your friends wisely

It is amazing how sometimes "You don't know what you've got 'till it's gone." (© Joni Mitchell) That's what happened when I thought I didn't save page 52 on the computer, and actually started to panic. Would that guided hand return?

I felt I was doomed! And then, with more searching and help from that man, the one with the beautiful brown skin (remember Ivor?) who now pushes all my wrong buttons, but is the only one who understands, has the know-how to get me out of a jam like this, and other ones. And, with a little prayer, I saw page 52 pop up. By the way, his name now is Theo, a.k.a. Ivor.

My concern is to not confuse you with what has come down in the last few years, after I left off writing in 2007.

So much has changed, yet the old feelings from my past are still there, but not as haunting, and with a new understanding.

I look at my bedside pictures of my mother in her later years, our heads butting. We look like the perfect mother and daughter——if only I could turn back time.

"Old way of thinking, Esther."

"Move on, girl...."

"Give it up to faith in your fate."

It seemed like overnight, the mother I knew turned into a helpless victim, throwing tantrums to get attention from Yanesh and me—at any cost. They lived in a retirement resort, with all the amenities, luxuries that most can't afford. The lovely condo that I bought for them in Leisure World, overlooking the city of Laguna Hills, California, had a beautiful flower garden and tennis courts that Yanesh so looked forward to every day.

As I look back and try to understand this woman, my mother, I see a little girl who used her looks and charm to capture victims into her web. Men were very drawn to her seductive ways. She had that "look"—blond hair, red lipstick, and a killer smile, a bit like Mona Lisa's "Come and figure me out." That was her M.O. to sustain her breath.

When she got a mild case of Parkinson's disease, to her it seemed as though she had terminal cancer. She got the sympathy (I felt) and it worked, for a while anyway. Poor Yanesh—active, handsome, loving Yanesh—ended up sleeping on the couch, while she would bang on the wall for even the smallest thing.

One day, when I saw her holding up her little hand mirror in bed and touching her face, it really shook me up. I stood there and just wanted to go over to her and tell her, "You are so beautiful, Mom." She would not believe me, as what she saw was no longer the woman with the spiked heels and long earrings, strutting down the runway, with all the hoopla.

And, making that grand, pool-side entrance, MISS VIENNA, where heads would turn, always ready to make that dive, but not into the swimming pool. Yet, I really cannot fault or judge her for her attitude, because I know that so many times I have done the same, in my own damaged way.

And what about Yanesh? If his daughters only knew that their father was wetting his pants, wearing spotted clothes, unshaven and barely speaking anymore, their papa who had bravely raised them without a mother, their articulate, kind father, an engineer, always with a newspaper or book in his hands, was now barely breathing life. Yanesh and I had a special relationship. He appreciated me, loved my singing voice, and would always say to my mother. "Rosie, vat a voice your daughter has."

"Yanesh, have you lost your hearing aid?"

Maybe those weren't the exact words, but that is what it felt like to me; the smile on his face spoke volumes. I appreciated Yanesh's wisdom and how deeply he cared about his daughters. He let me know in his own way that I was like a daughter to him; he tried to mend things between my mother and me.... He tried really hard in so many ways. How much more could he take?

If I closed my eyes....

Can't imagine why anyone would think Theo, a.k.a. Ivor, is my other half. Just because we speak on the phone about eight times a day and spend virtually 24/7 arguing, with him hanging up the phone on me for the dumbest reasons. To me he will always be Ivor, like I was "Estycoo" to my brother, Sam. Ivor, beyond his relentlessly creative sensibility, wise, personable, righteous, good-looking, sexy(?), loyal, devoted, and loves God. He is my best friend (sometimes), especially as my singing partner and when he creates beautiful songs for me to sing. His voice is to die for. We became a duo, a team, performing Puccini duets.

I think when I hear and watch him sing or hear him recite a piece of poetry he wrote in 18 seconds, those are the times I see him with my eyes closed, and my heart just feeling. Almost like when I first met him. I'm not sure if I really want to understand what I just wrote. Later…with Ivor.

One of Ivor's "18-second" poems: If I Closed My Eyes.

If I closed my eyes what would I see
I would see with my heart my soul
I would fall in love with every sense
That I have for so long ignored
Because my eyes are open
If I closed my eyes I would enjoy
The riches that
Every pore of my body was gifted with
Every cell that makes me who I am
If I close my eyes I could give up
Everything to the unknown
when I close my eyes for the last time,
I will see the divine intervening
To gather me up
For me to see the perfection
That created me
If I truly close my eyes with my eyes
Open, I know who I would be: a
divine Presence in a divine world.

I feel I have sort of, maybe in a scattered fashion, brought you up to date on my feelings of pain, joy, affection, love, and those who put me in a state of awe, more times than you could imagine.

Those were the times that gave me a brave enough heart to be candid and to continue; those were the times that inspired me to move on; those were the times I felt God speaking to me.

I never really quite understood "change...." Believe it or not, it is the "hair thing," that I kind of flippantly wrote about in the past (like my hair today never looks the same as yesterday, when I thought it was the best, especially highlights, like putting on make-up so it doesn't look like make-up, and now looks like make-up) that made me realize that no matter how hard you try, nothing is ever the same.... When I tried to get the same color, it became so clear to me, trying to get the same look back that there was an outer resistance and I felt the chatter in my head saying, "Move on girl, new day, give it up, re-invent...." Boy, did the creativity ever set in and keep me on my toes.

Would you believe the hair thing became an amazing catalyst for understanding change—it spilled over into other parts of my life. Who knew?

Only The Shadow Knows. (William B. Gibson)

"Give it up/give it over" (whatever/whichever) to let go of my yuck feelings that hold me back from feeling the possibility of something bigger, better to guide my vision, my dream, my everything. I am the "Leap of Faith" girl: mother, grandmother, friend, etc. I completely trust in something that has already been destined for me; it is so simple, yet I seem to forget what is, and has always been, right in front of my blind, sore eyes that brings me back——the beautiful trees, flowers, birds singing, the sun, the moon, the rain, and on and on and on. I am part of that beauty, in spite of it all (you know, the craziness).

What am I saying? My take is that we were born spiritual beings and everything we want to know, we already know. (Yes, a bit preachy, but that's the way I feel it.) I feel that God did not make me in His image, with the intention to be an empty shell and clueless. From my limited insight, I feel the thing they call " The Vibe" (gut trust)——the innate gift of intuitiveness guides our feelings, in collaboration with our guardian angels, both Earthly and in Heaven. Hang with me on this one.

So where am I going with this?

Oh, yes.... As life presents its challenges in all colors and shapes, I once again searched my heart and soul and had my conversations with my best friend (you know, the One I made my deal with).

But, not until I overdosed on the media—friends dragging me to seminars I really did not want to attend, but went because I felt I did not want to miss out on something. After all, one word to ponder at the right time can change one's life, even if just in a small way.

And, once again, same old, same old, same old, always turning to my collection of books, looking for new titles at my favorite new and second-hand bookstores, always coming back to the one I loved the most, next to me on my pillow. Remember that book that changed my life, been around for thousands of years and is the #1 bestseller of all time? After all, that's where it all began for me.

And then, talking to some of my wisest friends, especially my granddaughter, Dani, now all of nine years old (the other old soul, with the voice of an angel, sparkling eyes, and a smile that exudes love, love, love), I remembered who I am. I could have gone straight to the Source, always there for me, no appointments, no beating around the bush, no hula hoops or putting me on hold, the direct line to the One who orchestrated my life and gives all the answers (sometimes no answer is an answer). How simple is that? (Sure!) Once you get it, it sticks, right?

Meanwhile, between Carrie, David, my mom, her husband, Yanesh, my grandchildren, and the dog, and losing all my House of Cashmere stores in 1999, I moved my spiritual reading room from storefront to storefront, always in hopes of something good happening, or someone coming along and once again saving the day, as Steven Spielberg had.

As I was using all my own money (from Peter to Paul, Paul to Peter) to ensure the life of my vision and spiritual reading rooms, in 1998 I parlayed the Malibu ocean-front house that everyone loved, (except me, at the end) into a four-unit, 1927 Art Deco apartment building, coincidentally(?) sitting on the very same street where I grew up.

Now, in between the memories, plumbing, termites, vacancies, on and on and on, and the hair thing (lucky me, only 500 yards to Siren's, my rockin' hair salon), I live in the back in a converted garage, (that the kids call an outhouse—their hideout) so that I can still keep up with my work in progress, as they say....

P.S. Please understand. It's just a little ranting, not complaining; I am very grateful, always praying and making plea bargains with God.... It was always on my mind to refresh (like the Refresh and Delete buttons on my new toy). New ways and ideas to make things work even better. I always knew I would make a good think-tank partner.

I learned it from Sam.

I became a volunteer para-chaplain at a major hospital in Los Angeles. Friday was my favorite day to be the Sabbath-singing queen.

"Here she comes," the Rabbi would say.

It brings back warm feelings of how safe I felt when my father held my hand as we walked down Fairfax Avenue, squeezing it three times to give me our sign for "I love you." (Maybe that's where I originally got my "three times" thing.) Getting ready for our favorite day, Shabbas, with "challah" from Schwartz's bakery (no relation), another heartfelt connection that brings me back home.

Doing my work at the hospital was and is one of the most special days. When I entered the chaplaincy office, put on my badge, and the Rabbi said, "Go do your holy work, Esther," I felt a lump in my throat. I knew there were times when I felt so overwhelmed by life and the thought of walking into the rooms of terminally ill patients going into surgery, the families huddled, the families sitting apart, waiting for the diagnosis, frightened of The Unknown. When I enter a room and see no flowers, no balloons, no notes pinned up on the wall, I feel their pain, their emptiness, their loneliness and hope to give them the best of me—maybe some hope, maybe some solace, some wise words. I know those are the times that keep me coming back year after year....

At times when I knock on the door before entering, I think, "Who would want someone to come in and sing?" Words would be more appropriate, and besides, how many times can you say, "God will take care of everything?" Words don't come in pill form that you take every four hours, nor does anything else I could do. Getting ready to do a prayer on their behalf, I ask "What is your Hebrew name?" or "What is your given name?" I see their eyes well up with tears. I understand and just sing.

The feelings overcome me when I sing...

I feel I am with God,

so safe...so happy...so everything....

so good, so safe, so happy, so everything

Back to Theo, a.k.a. Ivor. He irritates me, irritates me, irritates me. He moves slow, thinks slow, smiles at everything, everyone, and charms people with his smile and bright white teeth (no whitening solution or braces, must be an India thing) and always has an answer that goes on for hours. He does not understand: "GIVE ME THE BOTTOM LINE, MAN, AND 'PLAN B'."

Yet when I call him 20 times a day, he listens until he does not like what he hears and hangs up. That's why I have to call him back 20 times, so I can get a word in and ask for his advice. He usually gives me the magic word or creative spark I need in order to move on.

Enough of Theo, a.k.a. Ivor for now. I now call him "Ive"' (Is there more to this than I know?) We don't understand each other's M.O. (forgot what that stands for, call Ivor...joke, joke).

It seems that whenever I start writing about Ivor, I mean Ive, memories of my mother, father, Sam, and others come up. Yes, I know what you're thinking, "Girl, you need help!" My help is doing just what I'm doing right now: trying to be useful, figuring things out. Maybe through writing my saga, I'll come to some realizations: one, that the mother-daughter thing is a universal theme, I am not alone—if only I knew this earlier.

The last visit to my mother and Yanesh's condo did it. What I saw, heard, and witnessed was like...I can't even find the words for how I felt.

Where is Sam? He promised we would grow old together. "Estycoo, I'm your 'bro,' "I take care of my 'sis.'"

"Okay, I NEED A SIGN; DO SOMETHING!"

This picture is too painful for me to see——my mother and Yanesh lying there like life is over. She doesn't even have her red lipstick on.

I called Yanesh's daughters and told them the situation. They came and whisked him off to Hawaii and I transported my mom to her new room in an assisted-living residence (resort type) around the corner from me.

I fixed up her room fit for a queen, all the colors she loved, a mirrored armoire/dressing table and a puffed-pink chair from the 1920s, like the old movie stars had. It looked like a boudoir, lined in black and gold. The mirror stretched out like an oriental fan, maybe more like a swan or an ostrich that flaunts its feathers. She could sit and primp all day long. I draped the curtains with lavender satin (she was very particular) and tied them back with big bows. I loved doing this for the mother I thought I hated. She became my Barbie doll. Unbelievable. I feel hope in this life.

David Steele, musician/rock star/manager/entrepreneur a.k.a. David Ungar, I think that's the only thing Theo, a.k.a. Ivor and him have in common—the a.k.a.s. Thank God for my son, David. I don't care HOW many a.k.a.s he needs.

David puts up with my 100 calls a day. What he does not know is that, "I just called to say I love you" (thank you, Stevie Wonder)" and to listen to his voice mail with the wonderful music he created, with his sweet voice singing. If only he believed in himself like I believe in him.... What he doesn't know is how often I lean on him for advice, and that I try to hold my calls to him until after his head-clearing hikes, like I used to do.

My granddaughter, Dani, gets me. We understand each other's vibe. When I look at her, I see my Carrie, my daughter, and remember how my father and I were the only ones who could hold her, or else she would cry. I still hold onto those feelings, even now when I get those polite hugs. Sometimes I stand there just to see if she'll reach out first, for once. Maybe one day, maybe at my gravesite, like I do now when I go to my mother's.... Rarely— too painful.

Revelation

Consider this:

All is possible

With your creativity

Your imagination

Your voice

Your hope

And God

In 1999, I was one of the first independent Cantors to pull together an interfaith Yom Kippur service in this most beautiful church, with a conservative Rabbi and the minister of the church. Mucho high ceilings, stained glass, if I could've, would've, could've moved in there, I would have been divinely happy. I can't imagine what my orthodox father would have thought.... I woke up that morning and could not move. I prided myself in creating my own High Holy Day prayer books. While bending over for six weeks at Kinko's in my high heels (a no-no), I dislocated something in my back. Over 100 bound pages, I made 400 prayer books in total. It was worth it.

My friend called me early in the morning on the day of Yom Kippur to tell me I was featured in the main section of the Los Angeles Times. I told her I couldn't move. She rushed over, looked at me, and said, "I have the best doc" and she drove me there at 5:30 a.m.

I had severe lower-back spasms, with unbearable pain going down my leg. In walks this guy in sweats, cut-off tank top, introduces himself: "Hi, I'm Dr. Perry. Go into the women's locker room and put on a swim suit." I thought, Is he serious? Little did I know who this man was. He put this contraption around me called a flotation vest with weights hung between my legs and on my ankles. He called this technique—he had invented it —"hydrokinetic spinal decompression," a method that opens up the spine, reducing pressure on the discs and pinched nerves.

He said, "Do as I say and you will be fine." His eyes were very direct. I felt safe. Then he dunked me in the pool for the day. After a couple of hours in the pool, I started to feel relief. I felt human again. I did not know who this Doctor LeRoy Perry really was. I found out later that he was the first official chiropractor to the Olympics, (like, five times).

3 p.m., still in the pool. . . . I had to sing the Kol Nidre at 7 p.m. I dared myself to test my voice in the pool, said a prayer, and took my chances. All of a sudden, the pain was, like, gone. It was as if the world stood still and I soared to Heaven. . . .

I looked around the swimming pool and realized it was surrounded by blocks of glass and high cathedral ceilings, as if the room were built to be a sanctuary to pray and meditate in. Dr. Perry told me afterward that when I sang, the other patients in the pool said they had experienced an unusual healing vibration.

He smiled. "I welcome you to sing here at ISI," he said, "anytime."

These were words I had longed to hear my mother say and for her to hear them from someone like Dr. Perry.

I told him I was afraid I would not be able to climb the stairs up to the pulpit to sing that evening. He put his hands on top of my head; I felt he was giving me a blessing (like the late Pope John Paul II had done to me from a distance). Looking straight into my eyes, he said, "You will sing."

He surprised me by coming to the church. I hobbled in with his contraption around my hips and stomach, with ice packs ready to be put into the pocket of the black belt wrapped around me (not the kind you win in karate). Just before the service, he even gave me another treatment! As I finished the service, I looked up and was even more surprised to see Dr. Perry still there, sitting on the balcony with his hands stretched out, palms up, giving me the thumb-up sign. I could not believe it. The celeb doc! After all, it was just little old me.

As destiny would have it, nine years later, 2008, I opened the House of Song, a.k.a. The SHUL at Dr. Perry's International Sportscience Institute. I am very lucky that I am doing my work, using my gift, my God-given voice, and that I became part of his triad of healing through the body, mind, and spirit.

I think my orthodox father and the nuns are smiling, and saying:

"Job well done." All this happened on a Friday,
my lucky day for miracles.

My lucky day for Miracles....

My voice became my calling card.

The fear still existed but it seemed that every time I opened my mouth to sing, even the fewest notes seemed to make people cry. How could I interpret this? All I was doing was my work, my love—to sing. Was there something they heard that I did not hear? Was it something they felt and saw that I did not see or feel? Remembering those early years, how I felt alone, it was like being transparent, an "almost life," always expecting a judgment call. Now they close their eyes and weep. I didn't know where they go emotionally, or what they are thinking, but they always came back, maybe healed or refreshed. At those times I, too, weep. I weep silently, in gratitude, in joy that my gift is having an effect, something is coming through me from the Source.... I just pray to do more of what I love to do the most—to bring people closer to themselves and to the Divine. I don't question this, nor should I.

I did a one-woman play about my life at an assisted-living home, and as I was acting out all the characters of my life and singing, I saw an elderly woman in tears. When I finished, she came over to me., "I have been carrying such torment and hate for my mother all my life," she said, "and now I can forgive her." The woman was 92 years old. I felt she got the blessing. I hope she finally forgave herself and her mother.

In order to fully live this life, I think we must express our God-given gifts, each in our own way, to feel complete, and then it will be a double blessing and will benefit others.

The Hebrew and the Latin —

the languages of the world

the poems

the enlightenment

the prayers

the moon and the stars

the wind and the rain

all encompassing

the Divine Source

of friendship

and love

make us who we are

your heart and your soul are within

your pure sight comes from inside you

Ivor became my Ive. There are times when I watch romantic movies like Gone with the Wind, When Harry Met Sally, and others, I recall the skip-of-the-heart feelings I had when I first met him, and fantasize him kissing me, holding my hand, and giving me "that look." I wonder if he, too, feels any of this, after all our emotional drama and me shutting him out of romantic intimacy.

Perhaps he feels as I do, that dedicating ourselves to a higher cause without the words being said spoke volumes of how he believed in and cared for me, with that relentless love he shows. I think back to all those years of him schlepping the audio equipment in his broken-down van to make it in time for our performances. And, how about when he got there, there was no help to bring in all that heavy stuff and set up? Then, half the time, he would forget a cord or microphone that was my favorite and disappear to get it and run back, not even enough time to change and feel good in fresh clothes, to sing with me. And what about all those times when I was even slightly sick, he would sleep at my bedside, on the floor? And how he sacrificed jobs that would have put food in his mouth, to make our usual deadlines. We went nuts big time, but everything always got done.

Lately, his face seems to be drawn. Maybe I expected too much of him (like mother, like daughter). But it's a good drawn, borne of 24/7 struggling to reach our goals. From the beginning, we both understood our coming together, that it was for a higher purpose, for which we were willing to sacrifice. Unspoken words. I always wanted him to shine and he wanted the same for me. I would even light one extra candle on Shabbas and talk to God about His servant, Ivor, to give him the blessing of singing his heart out…and oh my God, that voice…what a gift!"

When I first met him, he had dark hair. Now he doesn't even have time to dye it, but I do love that silver-gray outgrowth, and I hope he keeps it. Nix the pretty-boy look. He looks more mature, lovable, more seasoned.

I feel his distance from me. I guess it's to protect himself from feeling anything other than his commitment to getting our work done, so that all this will not have been in vain. I don't know what I feel; I'm too busy trying to fulfill my father's 1944 prophecy. Ivor feels he's my Earthly angel, helping me to fulfill my destiny, now our destiny.

Unbeknownst to him, I feel this is his destiny, to stand with me and sing in Hebrew, in Latin, sacred languages—me Jewish, him Catholic, evoking brotherhood through music, God's language. We do High Holy Days together, the Kol Nidre in harmony. By invitation, we have also done invocations at Buddhist temples, for people of Baha'i faith, as well as at worldwide gatherings of interfaith conferences, to sing and be of support to humanity.

One of our greatest highlights was being invited for an audience with, and to come back to sing for the beloved late Pope John Paul, II. After all these years, I am proud to stand with Ivor to do our thing. He always closes his eyes when he starts to sing with me and I feel his unconditional love for God and for what we do.

Between his composing beautiful melodies and lyrics for me to sing, and helping me to learn those Puccini arias to sing with him in Italian, guess who does all the handiwork to save me $$$ every time somebody moves out of my building?

Maybe he knows too much about me to feel that one day, anything could be different. Could I ever feel again those heartbeats like I did in the beginning?

Unforeseen destinies

From Ivor to Esther

How many years in a lifetime
How many lifetimes in a moment of pain
One word of kindness
One word to last forever
To keep in your locket of love

How much power in this girl's imagination
More worlds than the mind can fathom
One word would be enough
If it were yours to keep in your locket of love

The world has many stories
This is the story of Esther
Bound within bookends
Retraced with words
Steered in emotion
Written between lines
The images are priceless
Pages with covers is my story and my secrets
Of what was, what could have been, what is, and what should be

Esther...thank God for her gifts
Realized when I reached out
Knowing who you were
Opening the door to your freedom
Guiding you with a loving hand
You were my greatest secret, a great power
My secret is now a treasure for others to behold
Your life gracing the shelves of a bookcase
Facing a world of pain and courage
Never overcome by fear
Or deflected from your course of action
There is grace in life's jewels that are small
Worn and treasured
In my locket of love

This page is, for me, as a mother who adores her daughter, perhaps one of the most important pages. On it is why I wrote my story. I want to convey to other mothers and daughters the message and gift that my daughter, Carrie, gave to me. Luckily, I got this blessing just in time, before my story went to print in March, 2009, and before my time is up.

"You are not here with me in the present," my daughter said, "when I vent my stress, like studying for a major exam, like the kids are waiting for their dinner, like homework. You want to hear more, Mom?" What she doesn't understand is my M.O. when she shares with me her immediate plight and stress Immediately, I am thinking, how I can help her find solutions? Anything and everything just to help her out of the funk and give her some insight that, out of stress, she might have temporarily lost.

She says she wants me to be just a mother.

"What does that mean?" I ask her.

"JUST LISTEN."

The power of silence—no words.

Revelation

You are God's song

You are His delight

He is waiting for you to listen

To hear His still voice

Never too late to cry

Never too late to fix it

Never too late to mend it

2004

Many times a day, I ran over to my mother in the assisted-living residence around the corner. Being "Queen Bee" in her new home I thought would make her feel at home with herself. "Is there anything special my mother needs?" I asked one of her caregivers.

The caregiver looked at me, "You, Yanesh, different color eye shadow, more red lipstick, and who is that French captain who helped her to escape from the camp she was in?"

Strange that she should ask me that. I looked at the caregiver. What she asked was so simple, without knowing the ramifications of the doubts that surfaced about my birth, my father, and the way my mother was not the first person to hold me at birth. The doubts still linger, but my heart belongs to my father. If there ever was a time I felt like asking that question again, that time is too late——and does it really matter?

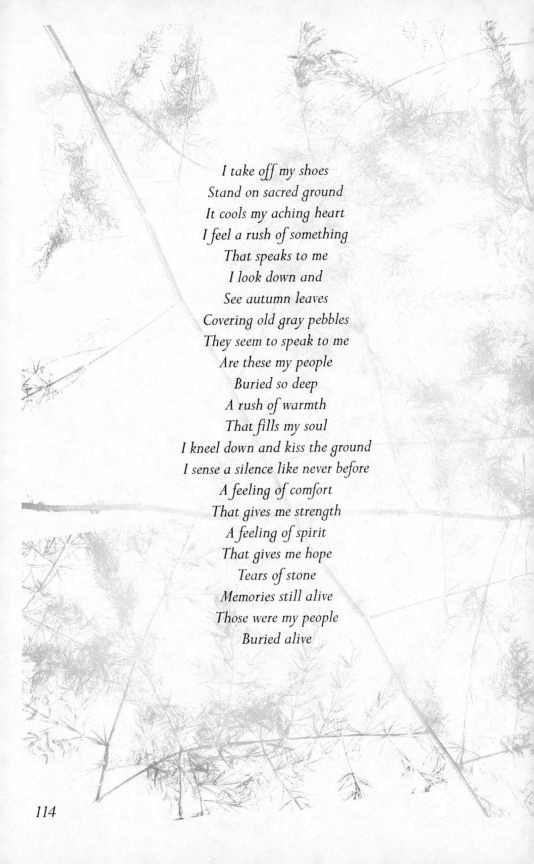

I take off my shoes
Stand on sacred ground
It cools my aching heart
I feel a rush of something
That speaks to me
I look down and
See autumn leaves
Covering old gray pebbles
They seem to speak to me
Are these my people
Buried so deep
A rush of warmth
That fills my soul
I kneel down and kiss the ground
I sense a silence like never before
A feeling of comfort
That gives me strength
A feeling of spirit
That gives me hope
Tears of stone
Memories still alive
Those were my people
Buried alive

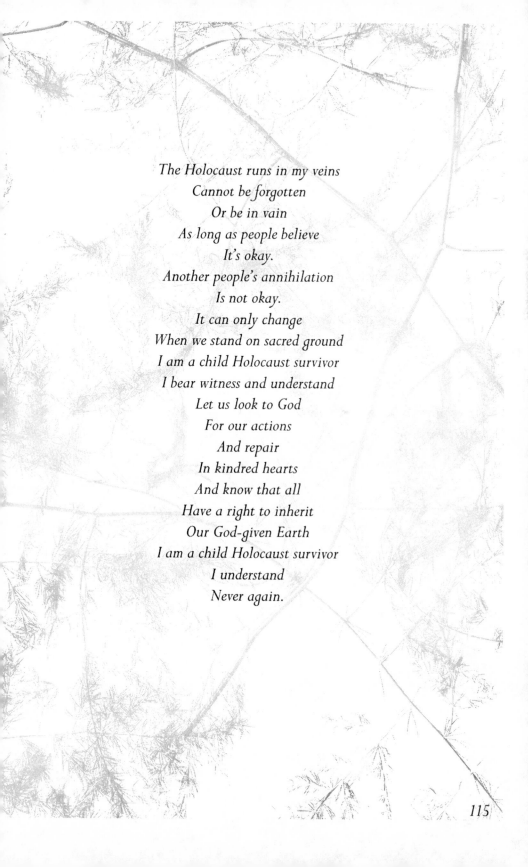

The Holocaust runs in my veins
Cannot be forgotten
Or be in vain
As long as people believe
It's okay.
Another people's annihilation
Is not okay.
It can only change
When we stand on sacred ground
I am a child Holocaust survivor
I bear witness and understand
Let us look to God
For our actions
And repair
In kindred hearts
And know that all
Have a right to inherit
Our God-given Earth
I am a child Holocaust survivor
I understand
Never again.

One day, my mother asked me to bring her to my place to live, as she was very lonely and wanted to be with me. She begged me. I thought of any excuse I could find to avoid this, (if only I had another chance to say, I'll get the movers), and at all costs, not move her into the empty unit, as Ivor (yes, Ivor) suggested I do. All I could feel at that time is NO, NO, NO. Still feeling the remnants of pain, and uncomfortable with how she still stared at me, reminds me of when Carrie says, "Stop staring at me." What she doesn't know is that it's the stare of awe, adoration, and love, like she stares at Dani, and maybe, just maybe what my mother might have felt for me (?).

Standing outside her room and looking in, I understood and saw a little girl missing her playmate, Yanesh. She was expecting him to miss her and hoping he'd leave Hawaii, where he was suntanning and getting lots of love from his daughters; and she was hoping he'd just pack up and arrive at her door #3-102.

I suppose she fantasized him saying, "Here, I am Rosie, my sweet little deer." Actually, she did look like a deer, with her high cheekbones and tiny nose. That delicate, helpless look that can destroy your spirit, and leave you lifeless, always needing more and more of that kind of attention....

Every day, she would ask me if he called or if a letter came from him. In those moments, my heart would ache for her; in the past, I have felt those feelings about some of my boyfriends; I felt so bad for her, for me, and for anyone else who goes through this.

So I started to make up stories. That "Yanesh just called when you were in the dining room; Yanesh just called when you were outside," on and on.... I even made up letters and read them to her and bought cards that said, "I love you, I miss you." She said, while looking in the mirror, "I tink he vill come back." I even made up that he had a light stroke and could not talk now, "but as soon as he gets better, he will join you.".....

Back on September 13, 2004, when I walked into her room, she was at the mirror cutting her bangs; her hands were so steady...she removed her big, shaded reading glasses and, as I got closer, I could see her deep, hollow eyes. I held back the tears.... I walked over and gave her a hug. She felt so tiny and looked so very happy putting on her red lipstick, and all the feelings of pain, anger, disappeared like magic. I told her I would like to have a mother-daughter talk later and she said, "Okay Esty, it's time." I felt it was the first time she looked at me in a non-judgmental way, that maybe she recognized my worth. And finally, at this moment I got the blessing, as they say.... She asked if I would do some special prayer songs in the recreation room for everybody. She even wanted for herself one of the prayer books I had made.

Unbeknownst to me, my CD has been playing in the dining room and people were coming over to her and saying: "You must be so proud of your daughter to have such a beautiful voice," and she would reply, "Yes, I am lucky to have such a daughter—and one who takes care of me like a doll! But don't compliment her too much; she might take herself too serious." My mother was still doing the same old stuff, but now it really didn't matter to me anymore. I was okay with myself.

As I was driving away to do a service, I thought about all the things I had always wanted to ask her in the past, about the escape and how it must have been so terrible to leave her mother behind, my grandmother telling her to, "Go, go," knowing she would probably never see her daughter again... I couldn't imagine such a thing or what she must have felt. I thought about how scared she must have been, seeing all those horrible things.... The separation from my father, being put into detention camp, what she must have had to endure—she was so beautiful.... I wanted to know about her escape with the French captain. And what about her unfulfilled marriage to my father? I just started to cry, the pain was too much. I stopped the car and tried to get my composure back. I asked God to help me. At that moment, I decided I was not going to ask her any of these questions. All I wanted to do was to let her know that I understood, and did not want her to feel guilty or ashamed of anything. I wanted her to know that I was happy to be her daughter and to be my father's child.

Later that afternoon, I came back with a prayer book for her—to an empty room. My cell phone had been off, as I was doing a service and did not get the emergency call from the hospital.

I held her lifeless, lily-white hand, ... and cut a piece of her blond locks; she was still wearing her glasses.... I removed them and just sat there. At times, I'm still sitting there.

I know she died of a broken heart, and now my pain turned into longing for her, just to have a chance to look at her and say,

"I love you. . . . ."

There is something greater

Above and around us

There is something bigger

That helps and guides us

Through our darkness

The intellectual

The spiritual quest

A cause and effect

Be in awe, seek, become

The child of inspiration

The child of poems

The child of songs

The joyous child

Of God

I did my mother's funeral service on September 16, 2004. I only invited those who came to see her in her "boudoir" and had cared for her: my cousins and my kids, Ivor and Phil, my ex-boyfriend.... It was more than pathetic how I had tried to share this woman's life, my mother, and our relationship. I held onto her wedding ring to give to Yanesh when I went to visit him in Hawaii. He looked like the old Yanesh I knew, tan, a newspaper in one hand, and a tennis racquet in the other. "She is still waiting," I told him. He looked at me with blank eyes and just smiled.... I gave him the ring...I saw him wipe a teardrop off his cheek.

He had to forget, in order to survive. Me too.

March 16, 2009, as I was finishing this last page, I got the call from Hawaii. My mother got her wish.... She no longer waits.

Esther's Revelation of Revelations...........

At long last, I finally understand my day-in-day-out longing for my mother.

I thought I never really got the kind of motherly love I needed. You see, not only did I miss out on the little things that mothers and daughters do, like I do with my Carrie — buy a new lipstick, have our nails done and listen to each other — over 3 zips at Starbucks. But even more than that, I didn't bring her to live with me in my little apartment, as she had begged me to do, to live out her days — even with her ragging on me — until she drew her last breath. It would have been so worth it.

The reason I have written this story is so that all you daughters out there will not have to go through what I did, swim such treacherous waters and drown in these tears.... Maybe, maybe I could have drawn from her the stories of her past, of my past, that she never got the chance to tell. I tried many times, but as I go over it in my heart, if we had lived together, spent all night talking, maybe they would have surfaced. Those stories, her story has now fallen through the cracks of history. My loss. But not forever.

When she passed on, I felt she left with a broken heart over Yanesh, leaving me in even more pain, since I, too, could relate to a broken heart. Now that Yanesh is with her, I'm happy for her. I feel my mother saying, "Esty, do your vork, ve help you, ve love you...."

When such words come from above, you just know. My mother is now giving me the motherly love she could not give me on Earth.

Better late than never....

Life can be beautiful
Life can be precious

Life can take you
Wherever you want to go

Life could be the window to your world
Where all you see is your destiny

Life could be precious
Life could be honorable
If you don't burn the bridges to you

Life could be precious
Life could be awesome

Go live for today
I'm thinking of you

There are all these treasures in your soul
There's always something that's good
To behold

And all that is coming into play
For you

Life can be beautiful, a bed to lie in
Or life could be a thorn of weeds

Life could be a miserable experience
Or it could be a jewel to cherish
I'm thinking of you

Life can be precious
Life has its own way of dealing with things
Life could be yours
What's yours is another choice

Mine is my choice
Mine has my meaning

Mine is the devil and angel questioning my reason
Mine is the motion burnt on the tongues of my life

Mine is the differences set for my day
Mine is the one and only experience

That I share with no one
I'm thinking of you
I'm thinking of you
I'm thinking of you

...

—— *From our CD, Respectfully Different*

   Estherleon and Ivor, a.k.a. Theo

A Message From the Author:

After finishing my story and getting it ready for print on a Friday, you know, my lucky day, I came to wonder what the point was of my writing it. It started out as a private letter to my children — I felt I wanted them to understand me better when it came to 'eulogy time.' But somehow my hand wouldn't stop writing. I shared some pages with friends and they asked, "Well, what happened next?" They started to share their own mother-daughter stories with me, at which point I realized I had a letter that wanted to be a book that could benefit relationships. Now I understand it is really a universal theme: the mother-daughter-relationship saga. The main point is for you to know you are not alone, as I thought I was. I encourage you to write your story, too, and you will get the blessing of fulfillment and healing.

This personal journey has taken me through many difficult stages in my life of 67 years, and I am happy I can say I have addressed so many necessary demons. In spite of everything and when it was all said and done, with a brave heart, I sang my way thru it all. With silent tears and a ton of prayers, I did it all.... It always was and still is my unconditional love for my children and grandchildren that keeps me grounded. And along the way came friends and a bigger picture — to serve humanity — always holding on to my father's words in 1944 at the Swiss border. Now, because I have resolved those demons, I've gained a new understanding, so I can elevate the work I love to do and be with you.

I became bi-coastal between Florida and Los Angeles. Through my concerts for humanity and this autobiography, I hope to reach as many people as possible. It is my wish and will be my privilege to donate $1 from the sale of each book which will go to FEED THE CHILDREN (Even if for no other reason, I hope I sell millions.)

Thank you, God — you gave me the chance to be me.

At present:

My deepest wish was to create a space for healing. I have fulfilled a long and cherished passion with the support of my friend, the respected Dr. LeRoy Perry. I am very grateful to have created the House of Song as a portal to inspiration and a pathway to awareness, self-expression and creativity, through the medium of the humanities, helping us to recognize beauty in this world, the love, the light in the people around us and within ourselves.

As a child holocaust survivor, the first years of my life on the run from the Nazis, sheltered in convents and small spaces constantly in hiding, made me realize how self-expression and freedom of thought are the most cherished needs of every human being. I became conscious that beauty exists in the most difficult circumstances and miracles are always possible when all seems hopeless.

A simple note of a song, the color of a picture, or one word heard in a workshop can, yes, spark your imagination, your God-given gift, to be realized through your passion and your burning desire. Your actions, my friend, can shift the consciousness of all humanity towards wellbeing.

The House of Song welcomes you to a safe harbor on your personal journey to a more enriched, abundant, and loving life; a place to nourish your soul and to gain the experience of the peace, balance and harmony that is your birthright.

The Music Department at International Sportscience Institute™
(ISI) provides a vital component of support for Dr. LeRoy Perry's Triad of
Health, Structural, Physiological/Nutritional, Psychological/Spiritual. With
leadership from the Dean of our music department, Howard Richman, and
a wonderful team of experts, a variety of music and sound applications are
brought forth. These include private sessions, listening room, evening concerts,
lectures, instruction and the Estherleon Schwartz House of Song music
meditation room. At ISI we believe music is an inspiration that can not only
enrich our lives as entertainment, but also as a modality for healing. As Dr.
Perry has said many times "Listen to your body, meditate. The music you hear
within is your gift. When your triad of health is in balance, the function of
your body, mind and spirit on all levels is in harmony. You are in a state of
homeostasis, steady state control, a state of ease. Just remember disease is a
loss of balance. So look deep within your inner space for your vibration, your
music, your peace and soon others will follow." —www.drleroyperry.com

Howard Richman, M.F.A., is a sound healing pioneer. Since 1982,
he has created more than 3000 individual sound portraits and composed
music for specific conditions. These include pain, stress, weight loss, cancer,
AIDS, depression, anger, birth, dying and dementia. Mr. Richman's specialty
is to help people break through their most stubborn blocks. He has a B.A. from
UCLA in piano performance and an M.F.A. (Master Fine Arts) degree from
California Institute of the Arts. —www.soundfeelings.com

Cantor Estherleon Schwartz, cantor, spiritual leader, community
leader who brings all cultures and religions together through her music and
concerts. She facilitates healing at a major hospital using her voice. It has
been said that her singing is "an embryonic experience for healing." She

officiates all life cycles and has private, spiritual guidance sessions at the House of Song.

On World Peace Day, September 21st, 2009, I was inducted onto the Board of Directors of the USA-Pacific Los Angeles Chapter of the United Nations Association. As an Ambassador for Peace, my intention is to continue our concerts: VOICES OF HOPE, CHILDREN HELPING CHILDREN — $1 of every book sold goes to aid FEED THE CHILDREN. To contact Estherleon for book signings and/or presentations, kindly visit the web site: —www.Estherleon.com

Ivor Pyres, *producer and director of concerts for VOICES OF HOPE, CHILDREN HELPING CHILDREN, in partnership with FEED THE CHILDREN. He is the creative director of visual arts, writer, producer, songwriter, blending music to heal the spirit, producer of all Cantor Estherleon's music, an avid photographer who tells stories with his photographs.*

Acknowledging just a few:

An hour before going to print, I called my cousin, my Monala, Mona Golabek, my mother's sister's daughter, who wrote the story about her mother called, The Children of Willesden Lane and is a world-renowned concert pianist. Mona is the only one left in the family, who, after all these years, I can talk to, to reminisce, and share all those memories of our family. Before any major decisions and the little ones, too, I call her. She became my brother in a way, and the sister I always wanted. When she completed the writing of her book, I asked her whether she experienced the feeling of: "I am ready to let this go," and she said, "Yes, Esty," I knew that what she said was what I needed to hear. Thank you, cookie-pie.

Michael Rosen, for all those hours of editing, formatting, your design, your patience, wisdom, and letting me know, "Enough with the. . . . ." To my final editor (who succeeded in getting rid of my dots), **Lisa-Catherine Cohen**: an unexpected angel once again came to me and, at the next last minute, guided me to a higher level of the craft, and for this, I thank you. You made it shine. —www.Lisa-Catherine.com. To Mara Quigley and Steve Allen, my PR team, thank you for giving me endlessly of your time and know-how, taking Tears of Stone And My Deal With God to its widest audience! —www.SteveAllen media.com. To **Pascale**, for enlightening me as to what was missing in the early stages of the book, and for your kids' input on the book's cover in between doing their homework, eating dinner, and watching TV; **Maurice**, for the hours of putting up with me and Ivor in the recording studio and for taking my post-dated checks; **June**, thanks for reading the book and giving me your thumbs up; **Linda**, your quantifying one sentence and how one word made the world of difference and made me look good; **Daryl**, always bringing flowers from your sacred garden to our music gatherings; **Sandy**, for your magical artistry, improvising on canvas the essence of the music; **Mana** and **Laura**, bringing me back when I think I've lost it; **Gloria**, a.k.a. Glor, "Girl, you made me laugh and cry at the same time;" **Larisa**, when I first started to dictate my story, I remember your fingers typing away. . .and thank you, too, for lending your most beautiful art to our walls in our meditation room; **Pasqual**, I thank you for always saying just the right words to remind me who I am, and for playing my CD in your Museum of Art; **Joseph** at **WH Printing**, for accommodating me, even if you had already closed shop; **Starbucks**, on Stanley and Melrose, *for all the loving refills;* **Rebecca Runze,** *our chocolate connection.* **Joy,** *for opening our meditation room each morning with such loyalty;* **Sharon,** *for your insights and our "mother connection";* **Howard Richman,** *thank you for playing the piano, improvising and challenging me to improvise, flying with you into another world;* **Joe Stern,** *for lending me the Matrix Theatre for High Holy Days and for loving Ivor;* **Meredith,** *at Sirens, my rockin' hair salon for understanding my hair thing and the good, worldly talks;* **Norma Foster,** *for guiding me me to become a Board member of the UN, Los Angeles chapter, and including me in world invocations;* **Joanna,** *for all your gifts, your relentless caring in these difficult times, yet letting me know that when I sing a cappella, you feel God;* **Mabel,** *your book inspired me to write mine and for always looking out for me for introductions;* **Joycie,** *for our history together and my leaning on your saving-grace words;* **Maureen,** *for always watching over me in getting the word out;* **Richelle,** *Thanks, cookie, for believing in me from day one.*

And, to all those whom I have not yet met, who come to sit in our MUSIC meditation room, I hope one day to meet you. When I'm alone there, I do feel your essence and your spirit.

To my Lynnie: You are my true connection to Sam on this Earth....
When I hear your voice, I see him and hear his voice. I am so proud of the
boys. Sam must feel so good to see one of his sons is a policeman and involved
in a community hot line — a special program that saves lives — and his
other son, a college basketball coach, inspiring kids to challenge themselves,
who is now a father of two beautiful daughters. They call themselves "The
Schweez Brothers."

Sam's youngest son, from his second wife, is an artistic director,
computer guru, and an aspiring movie producer, already winning festival
awards. One day, we will all be together again.... like when I held you all
when you were young. Your pictures have always been at my bedside. Love,
Auntie Esty.

RESPECTFULLY
dIFFERENT

Estherleon & Theo

As with the rest of my life, destiny always shaped itself at the last moment. Just as we go to print, I have been asked to sing at the Hollywood Bowl for the 88th annual Ecumenical Easter Sunrise Service, on April 12, 2009.

Thank you, Mom, Dad, Sam, thank you God...
I am beginning my own resurrection.....

I stand across the street
Looking into my house

I see characters
That
I thought I knew

My mother, My father
My daughter, My son
My best friend
And most of all
Now, me

Me... out of myself
Out of my skin

I stand across the street
Looking in
Me... the main player
Seeing in

Who are these characters
I thought I knew?

Always the same character
Me...
that I thought I knew

My mother, My father
My daughter, My son
My best friend

They look and feel
Different in so many ways

Was I in the way of myself?

...A different perspective
To learn and understand
I still have a chance
From mindless choices
That gave me pain

To turn them into
Jewels of understanding

They too had their pain

I stand across the street
Ready to knock on the door

Tears of endearment
On my heart
I've come home...

...Different choices
Now I make
Always remembering
My deal with God